Empty Pockets and Full Plates:

EFFECTIVE BUDGET ADMINISTRATION FOR LIBRARY MEDIA SPECIALISTS

Gail K. Dickinson

Linworth Publishing, Inc.
Worthington, Ohio

Acknowledgements

Every author needs a technology expert. I am grateful for the help of Alex Colson, who created graphics, fixed computer glitches, and in so many ways cleared the technological problems that happened. I also acknowledge the support of my daughters, Maggie and Beth Ann, for their constant encouragement.

Dedication

To Mike

Library of Congress Cataloging-in-Publication Data

Dickinson, Gail K.
    Empty pockets and full plates : effective budget administration for library media specialists / Gail K. Dickinson.
       p. cm.
    Includes bibliographical references and index.
    ISBN 1-58683-056-2 (perfect bound)
    1. School library finance--United States. 2. Library materials budgets--United States. 3. Instructional materials centers--United States--Finance. I. Title.

Z683.2.U6D53 2003
025.1'1--dc21
                                                     2003040093

Published by Linworth Publishing, Inc.
480 East Wilson Bridge Road, Suite L
Worthington, Ohio 43085

Copyright © 2003 by Linworth Publishing, Inc.

All rights reserved. Purchasing this book entitles a librarian to reproduce activity sheets for use in the library within a school or entitles a teacher to reproduce activity sheets for single classroom use within a school. Other portions of the book (up to 15 pages) may be copied for staff development purposes within a single school. Standard citation information should appear on each page. The reproduction of any part of this book for an entire school or school system or for commercial use is strictly prohibited. No part of this book may be electronically reproduced, transmitted, or recorded without written permission from the publisher.

ISBN: 1-58683-056-2

5 4 3 2 1

Table of Contents

List of Figures iv
Part 1: Introduction 1
    Chapter 1: Management and Administration of the School
               Library Budget Process 5
        Change Processes 7
        Visioning 9
        Implementing Your Vision. 12
    For You to Do 12
    What Would Savvy Library School Media Specialists Do? 13

    Chapter 2: School Library Media Budget History. 15
        Pre-History—Before 1960 15
        The 1960s and the Early 1970s. 17
        Post-1975 22
        Historical Data and Statistics 24
            Statistical Procedure. 27
            Library Media Book Expenditures. 28
            Other Materials. 30
        Summary 32
    For You to Do 32
    What Would Savvy Library School Media Specialists Do? 38

    Chapter 3: Understanding the Budget Terms and Processes 39
        How the Money Gets There 40
            Effect of School Reform 45
            Type of Budgets 49
                Zero-Based Budgets 49
                PPBS: Planning, Programming, Budgeting System 50
                Performance Budgets 51
                Percentage Increase. 53
            The Budget Timeline 53
        The Big Picture. 54
            When Government Plays a Market Role 56
            Production Function Economics 56
                The School Library Media Production Function 59
                Funding Adequacy 60
                Funding Equity 61
        Summary 62
    For You to Do 63
    What Would Savvy Library School Media Specialists Do? 64

Table of Contents *continued*

Part 2: Planning 65
    Chapter 4: The Importance of Advocacy 67
        What is Advocacy? 70
        Why Me? 76
        Summary 77
    For You to Do 78
    What Would Savvy Library School Media Specialists Do? 79

    Chapter 5: How Much Money is Needed? 81
        Mandates and Standards 86
            Regional Accrediting Associations 88
            State Standards 90
        Beyond the Standards 90
            Staff 91
            Facilities 92
            Collection 93
        Collection Analysis Procedure 94
            Books 97
            Audiovisuals 98
            Equipment 98
            Other Resources 99
        Summary 99
    For You to Do 100
    What Would Savvy Library School Media Specialists Do? 100

    Chapter 6: Adding Dollars to the Budget Picture 101
        Gathering Financial Data 104
            Books 105
            Audiovisuals 107
            Other Resources 109
        Establishing the Bottom Line 109
        Developing the Maintenance Budget 111
        Summary 113
    For You to Do 113
    What Would Savvy Library School Media Specialists Do? 114

Table of Contents *continued*

Part 3: Putting the Plan Together 115
    Chapter 7: The Budget Presentation 117
        Writing the Budget Presentation 119
            Introduction to the Presentation 119
            Overall Justification 123
                Question 1. What's in It for Me? 123
                Question 2. How Do You Know What I Need? 123
                Question 3. What Will Happen If This Plan Becomes
                    Reality? 124
            Budget Body 124
                Books 125
                Magazines 125
                Audiovisual Materials 126
                Electronic Resources and Computers 127
                Supplies 128
            Budget Summary 128
        Budget Implementation 131
            Before Beginning 131
            Making the Presentation 132
            After the Presentation 133
            Presentations Without Presenting 133
            Other Tips 133
        Summary 134
    For You to Do 135
    What Would Savvy Library School Media Specialists Do? 135

    Chapter 8: Other Issues of Budgeting 137
        The Value of Time 137
        Fund Raising 138
        Grants 139
        Gifts and Donations 140
        Other Department Budgets 140
        Summary 141

    Chapter 9: Furthering the Vision 143

Appendix A 147
Glossary 151
Bibliography 155
Index 161
About the Author 163

List of Figures

1	The Budget Cycle	2
1.1	Some Introductory Behaviors for School Library Media Specialists	8
1.2	Visioning Exercise	10
2.1	Behavioral Requirements Analysis Checklist Excerpted Tasks	19
2.2	Committee for Full Funding	20
2.3	Sampling of 1980s of Literature	23
2.4	Mean Collection Size, 1958-2000	25
2.5	Mean Collection per Pupil, 1958-2000	26
2.6	Historical Overview of School Library Media Book Expenditures	28
2.7	Books Purchased per Pupil	29
2.8	Trend Analysis of Non-Book Resources (Elementary)	30
2.9	Trend Analysis of Non-Book Resources (High School)	31
2.10	Spreadsheet Worksheet	33
2.11	Spreadsheet Worksheet (Revised)	34
2.12	Current Dollar Calculation	35
2.13	Completed Spreadsheet	36
3.1	Budget Functions	42
3.2	Budget Codes	43
3.3	Relationship of the Site-Based Management Team and the School Library Media Budget Process	47
3.4	Comparison of School Library Media PPBS Budget	50
3.5	Performance-Based School Library Media Programs	52
3.6	School Library Media Production Function	59
3.7	The Budget Cycle	65
4.1	What Does Your School District Value?	68
4.2	Advocating the Vision	72
4.3	Advocacy Overview	74
5.1	School Library Media Production Function	83
5.2	Filters at the School Level	85
5.3	Comparison Chart of National Guidelines	87
5.4	Sampling Comparison of Regional Accreditation Standards	89
5.5	Budget Needs	96
6.1	Budget Worksheet	103
6.2	Finding the Average Price per Item for Library Materials	105
6.3	Expenditures for Audiovisual Materials	108
6.4	Alternative Spreadsheet Example	110
6.5	Preparing the Maintenance Budget	112
7.1	Alignment of the School Library and School Missions	120
7.2	Values and Beliefs Worksheet	122
7.3	Frequently Asked Questions about Library Budgets	129
7.4	Budget Presentation Plan Overview	130
9.1	The Budget Cycle	144

Part 1

Introduction

"If I Had a Million Dollars?" ... is the tune and title of a popular rock song. However fanciful the lyrics, school library media specialists often speculate about money, what they could do if they had some, how little they actually have, and how much more they need. The school library media budget allocation tests the degree of support that the school district gives to the school library media program.

This book is an in-depth look at the development process for the school library media budget cycle. It is not a book on grant writing, book fairs, or alternative funding. Rather, this book is written for school library media specialists serious about changing the budget environment within the school and district to be one of stable support for school library media programs.

Figure 1 shows the graphic of the budget cycle, which reflects the organization of this book. As with true repeating cycles, there is no starting or ending point. The budget cycle is a repeating spiral with new knowledge making deeper planning possible, which impacts implementation, creating new knowledge once again. It is a true spiral, with all parts of the budget process happening at the same time.

Figure 1: The Budget Cycle

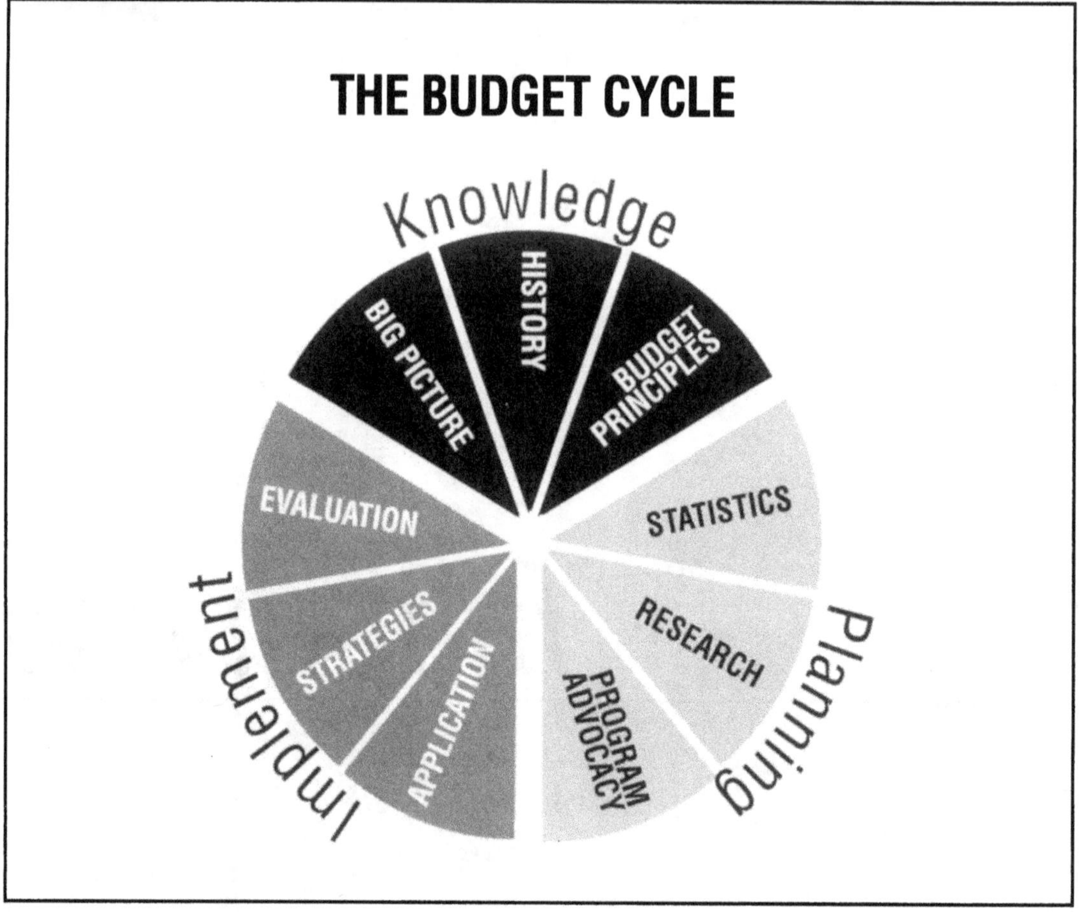

THE BUDGET CYCLE

Knowledge: HISTORY, BUDGET PRINCIPLES, BIG PICTURE
Planning: STATISTICS, RESEARCH, PROGRAM ADVOCACY
Implement: APPLICATION, STRATEGIES, EVALUATION

Part 1 of this book reviews background knowledge needed for successful budget planning. The three chapters in this part are an overview to the issues involved in school library media budgeting. In the first chapter, information on creating change is presented. In order to understand the financial evolution of school library media programs, Chapter 2 is a look at our history and at how the ebb and flow of funding streams in our past have impacted school library programs in the present. The third chapter is a look at school district finance philosophy and procedures and an overview of budget principles, terms, and methods.

Part 2 covers the development of a budgeting plan. This development process is divided into three chapters. Chapter 4 reviews the data available at national, state, and local levels, including statistics available in your school district on school library media budget allocations. These statistics will guide your budget development as you read further in Chapter 5, which takes you through the process of developing research data to apply to your local situation. Chapter 6 helps you identify the power players and power strategies in the district, and how to advocate for your program with the right people and at the right time to get your point across.

Part 3 covers the implementation of budgeting strategy. To achieve implementation, a budget plan has to be developed, complete with timelines. The plan must be multi-dimensional, focusing as much on program as it does on dollars. Alternative funding sources are the focus of Chapter 8. In Chapter 9, the plan is pulled apart as the budget is redesigned, including recording budget successes, evaluating, and rethinking the budget plan.

Make no mistake; implementing sound budget strategy is a lot of work. However, the rewards can be great. As you work through the processes and strategies, you will find that it is difficult to remove budget development processes from the normal administrative routines of the library. Most likely, you write reports as a normal routine, send newsletters to teachers, and talk to parent groups. Advocacy is a daily part of the routine for strong, high-service library media programs. The budget process simply focuses those activities with a definable goal; it is not couched in terms of what this will do for the room, the building, or even the collection. The purpose of budgeting for the library media center program is to create a positive effect on the teaching and learning processes in the school. Time is precious, and we only have one chance to influence the lifelong learning of students at each grade level. The steps outlined in this book will maximize that time and effort and will keep the focus directed toward student learning and achievement.

This book is not about a one-time initiative. You may do a collection analysis and find that to bring your collection up to speed, you may need an allocation of $15,000. The school district can decide to update information technology and spend double or triple that amount on each school library media center. Although this certainly may help immediate concerns, it has almost always has a negative effect in the long term.

The problem with one-time allocations, as we have found in the past with computer technology bond issues, is that once the initial money has been spent, the job is presumed to be finished, and the school board may be reluctant to continue to allocate funds. ("We just spent ALL that money.") It is far better to initiate a budget stream that can be repeated every year and that, over time, can achieve lasting results. Corn doesn't grow under Niagara Falls. A slow steady rain is the best way to irrigate crops. Creating a stable process that will provide maximum growth and benefit for students and faculty is what this book is about.

Chapter 1

Management and Administration of the School Library Budget Process

"Mom, I need 20 dollars."

"Twenty dollars, for what? What happened to the 20 dollars I gave you yesterday? Money doesn't grow on trees, you know."

This reminiscence of teenage years is the basic premise of budgeting in the accountability age. Just like the teenager in this dialogue, school library media programs need money to function. And, most likely as the teenager above does, we may think the answer should be perfectly obvious. We need books, computers, licenses, furniture, and many other elements of a modern school library media program. Why isn't it obvious that libraries need money to function?

Valid complaints about a lack of attention to the funding needs of the school library media program will always surface in conversation around meeting tables at conferences and in the literature of the school library media field. However, while raising lack-of-support issues, we still should be prepared to answer questions very similar to those the harried mom is asking in the dialogue that introduces Chapter 1.

Why do school libraries need money to function? What has been the impact of the money expended in years past on school library programs, both at the building level and nationally? And, importantly, in times of uncertain economic strength, what research, statistics, and other data can we gather to show how our funded mission is central to teaching and learning processes in the school?

It has been difficult to miss the emphasis on accountability for the public schools. Recent interest in voucher systems and expanded testing at each grade level has forced schools to reexamine how they are using instructional time and instructional resources. The pressure on classroom teachers and principals is enormous, as test results may not only determine the graduation or promotion of students, but in some states, also may determine the continued employment of the classroom teacher or building administrator. Low-performing schools are identified publicly in most states and are forced to change in some way in an attempt to improve performance.

These changes do not always benefit the library media program, even when the improvement clearly targets initiatives, such as reading or information technology. If a school needed to improve reading test scores, it would be logical that the school library media program would be the recipient of funds for increased collections, improved facilities, and increased staff. This rarely happens. Even worse, sometimes library staff positions are cut, support staff is reassigned, or collection development funds are redirected to purchase computerized reading systems or other initiatives. Even more common is the situation where thousands of dollars are directed to establish classroom libraries, while the library media program has to hold book fairs to raise money for the magazine budget.

On the other hand, it is also clearly untrue that school library media centers are always forced to do without needed funds. There have been major technological innovations that have changed not only the way that school library media centers operate but have also changed the appearance of school libraries. Almost all library media centers are automated. Where did the money come from to buy computers for automation and for electronic information resources? Perhaps the upkeep and yearly expenses fall to the library budget, but later chapters will show that the initial money in most cases was found elsewhere. Even in the last several decades, with little federal assistance and uncertain local funds, school library media programs obtained computers, networked them, purchased information technology resources, and automated collections. Obviously, money existed.

As a field, we must accept that school library media programs have operated, for the most part, outside the pressure cooker of accountability. We empathize with grade-level and subject-area teachers as they march their students in double-time to the testing date, knowing that failure has drastic consequences for students, teachers, and administrators. There is no end-of-year information literacy skills test that would determine the staffing level, budget, or management of the library media center. Our budgets are usually not affected by a single high-stakes test. But what if such a test existed? Would school library media programs operate differently if the bullets of high-stakes testing were aimed at our mission? Probably, and we probably should act as if they were.

To move from what you have to what you want means change has to occur. The budget wheel processes of knowledge, planning, and implementation cannot start turning in a static environment. To start thinking about the budget process in schools, we have to begin by thinking about change.

Change Processes

All change is personal. Your library media program should occupy an active, vibrant place in the budget process and should be involved in most of the instructional efforts in the school. If this does not describe the current place of the school library media program, then the perception of the library program held by students, teachers, administrators, and parents may have to change. And for that to happen, you have to change. An important part of the self-esteem initiatives of the recent past is based on the following three principles of change (Canfield, 1993).

- People can change.
- You can't change people.
- You can only change your response, and therefore create an environment in which change can occur.

You can't directly affect the behavior of others. All you can do is change your response; in other words, to change the environment so that people can change. Too many times we have heard endless complaints that the principal is not supportive or that classroom teachers have had no training in school library collaboration. Continuing the cycle of complaining about the behaviors of others, yet reinforcing those behaviors by our continuing passivity, will change nothing.

Remember that changing your response to a situation is the only thing you have under your control. Stephen Covey, in his popular "Seven Habits" series, talks of the circle of influence and the circle of control. As you work to change things that you control and to create opportunities for change to occur where you have influence, you can also create opportunities for change to occur outside your sphere of influence (Covey, 1990, p. 82). Covey talks of the circle of influence and the circle of control. Covey notes that as you concentrate on creating change on what you can control, you can increase the areas in which you have influence. Concentrating on the circle of control increases the circle of influence.

Creating a situation in which change can occur may mean that you may have to change your belief system about how you operate the school library media center. You may have to take on attributes and behaviors that are new and different for you.

One of the responses most commonly heard about budgeting is that the school library media specialist has no control over the amount of money allocated to the school library media program. That is only partially true. You have total control over how much money you request. Requests could possibly lead to increased funding. The difference lies in taking control of the influence you could have rather than allowing others to control you. Which would you rather do?

Change means that you may have to adopt some behaviors new to you. To get you started in identifying behaviors that you may have to change, look at the checklist in Figure 1.1. Check the behaviors that you feel adequately describe your interaction in the library media center.

Figure 1.1: Some Introductory Behaviors for School Library Media Specialists

- ☐ I keep detailed records of budget expenditures.
- ☐ I write monthly newsletters to teachers and a monthly report to the principal.
- ☐ I follow up newsletters with personal notes and visits to teachers' classrooms.
- ☐ During my annual evaluation with my administrator, I do most of the talking.
- ☐ I serve on most curriculum committees within the school.
- ☐ I have a good relationship with the school support staff, especially the school secretary and the custodian.
- ☐ It is rare that during a meeting I don't have something to say.

Look at Figure 1.1. Notice the behavioral characteristics of thoughtful organization, self-confidence, and an understanding of the value of the school library media program in the school. Pay particular attention to the behaviors that indicate a willingness to speak out for the program, not in the library workroom or teacher's lounge, but in places where decisions are made. These are the characteristics needed to run a strong library program. What if you do not have the opportunity to serve on any committees, if the principal does not evaluate you, or if you don't do monthly reports or newsletters? Then that is a good place to start. Occasionally, a principal who is new to a school may walk into the library, express shock and horror at the low funding level, and might immediately quadruple your budget, with promises of more staff, new facilities, and further increases in budget for years to come. Although that may happen, it is probably more likely that you will slowly and thoughtfully have to present program and budget information to convince your principal and others in the school that dollars spent on the library program help to educate every student.

What about fund raising, grant writing, book fairs, and other alternative ways of finding money for library programs? Yes, those can be extremely important, but the school district has a responsibility to fund the library program out of taxpayer funds, just as it does any other instructional program. It is unheard of for the math department to hold a fund raiser so that it is able to offer advanced algebra classes. Even for a new initiative, such as advanced placement calculus, the strategy is to convince parents, administrators, the school board, and taxpayers that the children of the community are lacking the benefits that the new program will provide. In general, the math department tries to convince decision makers of the value of the new program, rather than assume that the value is so hidden that they will have to raise the money themselves.

John Dewey said it best:

I believe that the community's duty to education is, therefore, its paramount moral duty. By law and punishment, by social agitation and discussion, society can regulate and form itself in a more or less haphazard and chance way. But through education society can formulate its own purposes, can organize its own means and resources, and thus shape itself with definiteness and economy in the direction in which it wishes to move. (Dewey, 1897; Dworkin, 1959, p. 31)

It is the duty of the community and the school district to fund school library programs. It is your responsibility to create avenues for that to happen. The first step is to articulate your vision for the library media program.

Visioning

Creating, articulating, and sustaining a vision is the subject of several excellent books and articles for school library media specialists and other educators (Allen, 2001; Carver, 1997; Crowley, 1995; Kearney, 2000). For more in depth study, you may want to consult one of those or another process used in your district. Briefly, a vision is a statement of the future on which specific goals can be built. It illustrates the intentions of an organization and paints the picture of what life would be like in the organization if the vision is achieved.

In order to begin the change process in the library, you have to create at least the basic framework of a strong and articulate vision. A good place to start is to reread the beginning chapters of *Information Power* (AASL/AECT, 1998). Pay particular attention to the strength of the mission, "to ensure that students and staff are effective users of ideas and information" (p. 6). Now think about the library program in the school. Write down some words and phrases that you think describe your most basic beliefs and values about the school library media program in your school. This will be a starting place for your vision.

The activity in Figure 1.2 may help you to begin to think about your vision for the school library media program. This is a brief synopsis and a beginning exercise. There are many books available on visioning, both in education and in librarianship. You may want to search for one, and then at a later date, do a more thorough vision-building experience.

Figure 1.2: Visioning Exercise

Visioning Exercise

1. Write down some words and phrases that "deep down" represent what you feel about the interaction of students and libraries. _____
   _____
   _____

2. When you go home thinking, "this was a good day," what happened to make you feel that? _____
   _____

3. Read the first chapter of *Information Power*. Write the mission of the library media program here. _____
   _____

4. Your school district has a mission statement. Write it here. _____
   _____
   _____

5. Your school most likely has a mission statement as well. Write it here. _____
   _____
   _____

6. Now look at the words on this page. Circle the ones that mean the most to you. ____
   _____
   _____

7. Develop a rough draft of your mission statement. _____
   _____
   _____

8. Now think about this rough draft. How will you know that you have achieved it? What will students and teachers be doing? If the superintendent walked in your door, what would you like him or her to see to know that you have achieved this?
   _____
   _____
   _____
   _____

Remember, the work does not end when a vision is created. The vision only creates the destination. The mission statement is the concise articulation of the vision. The strategies are then a road map that can be matched against the vision and the mission to determine if they will be helpful to reach the end of the road.

Dyson and O'Brien, in their edited book on Strategic Modeling, list the following elements of successful visioning (Dyson & O'Brien, 1998, p. 37):

- **Motivation for Change**—Is there a need for change? Are you satisfied with the library program as it is? Or are there elements that stand in the way of excellence in library programming? For many library programs, one of the greatest barriers is lack of a stable funding source. To what extent is a lack of funding a motivation for change?
- **Participation**—Dyson and O'Brien note that while it is possible for an organization to have a strong vision created by one person, such as Walt Disney or Bill Gates, most organizations gather people whose daily work lives would be affected by the vision to reach consensus on the direction. The school library media field has many energetic, enthusiastic, and charismatic leaders at the building level who are creating great change. However, change that is created by the energy of one person tends to leave with the person. It is better to create a deep level of support for the program across the organization, rather than focused within a specific person. Deep levels of support happen when there is a wide diversity of participation in the mission of the school library media program.
- **Focus on Values**—The literature of the school library media field provides infinite fodder for discussion of the important values underlying our profession. Chapter 1 of *Information Power* (AASL/AECT 1998) is a great place to start. Read through it again with a highlighter in hand. What words or phrases evoke an emotional response as you think about your program?
- **Communication**—Are the elements of your vision shared? Do classroom teachers feel that you listen to them, that you understand their work? Communication must be two-way; first you listen, then you talk.
- **Commitment to Action**—Why prepare a vision if you do not intend to work to achieve it? After the hard work of preparing a vision, can you ask those who have invested time in preparing it to work for it? If truly invested in the vision, most will say yes, especially if they know that you are leading the effort.
- **Vision Versus Present State**—If you survey the members of the learning community who access the library program, many will probably say that the library media program provides excellent service. Other than simply wanting to be nice, most would say this because they truly do not know what they are missing. You will need to show why the present state of affairs is not what it could be. Note that this will lead back to the beginning of this cycle ... the motivation for change.

Implementing Your Vision

There are many words and phrases that are used as slogans to describe the impact of school library programs. "Kids who read ... succeed," from the American Library Association (ALA), is an example of one of these highly successful images (ALA, 2002). The slogan is succinct, yet carries a strong message. What is the vision of your school, of your school district, of your community? Can you add some phrases to your vision from the mission statements of other organizations?

In their research on "Library Power," Douglas Zweizig and Dianne McAfee Hopkins noted that success happened much easier when the inquiry-learning emphasis of "Library Power" meshed with the existing vision of the school (Zweizig & Hopkins, 1999, p.191). Your school may already have a mission statement that includes reading, information literacy, or inquiry. Showing how the library program can support the mission of the school helps to strengthen your mission and makes the library program appear more central to the instructional life of the school.

When working through the exercises in future chapters, it will help to have the beginnings of a strong vision in hand. You should be determined that although you will do your part with grants, book fairs, and other means of funding, it is the duty of the school board and the community to fund fully the library media program as part of their responsibility for the learning of the community's young people. After all, if you allow them to feel as though they are not responsible, you've taken away part of their reason to keep you around. Most importantly, if you really want your budget to match your vision, you will have to change your behaviors and your responses to the behavior of others.

Ask yourself, are you ready for change?

Re-think the vision and the mission of your school library program. If you don't have one, begin the steps to construct that meaningful foundation. We will be returning again and again to the mission and the vision.

Translate your vision and mission into practical application. What does it mean to your students and faculty that you are working to "ensure that students and staff are effective users of ideas and information?" What evidence do you have that you are working to achieve that mission?

Decide to work for improvement. The steps in this book will be some degree of work, but will have good consequences. Make your decision, and then tell someone else what you are going to do.

What Would Savvy School Library Media Specialists Do?

Savvy school library media specialists post the mission. Banners that stretch from one end of the library to the other proclaim your dedication as well as the reason why you do what you do.

Savvy school library media specialists use the "I-" word. They teach people how to find information, but more importantly, they teach people how to use information. Information skills, information resources, and information access stretch the library media program across grade levels and overshadow previous stereotypes of library skills worksheets and shushed students.

Savvy school library media specialists talk about their vision and mission. They want. They want the school library media program to be an invaluable resource. They're idea people. They're action people, and they always seem to be in the thick of each activity. Nonetheless, they know they can't be everywhere all the time, so they make sure that others know the vision and the mission. Savvy school library media specialists let others know what they expect for the library media program.

Chapter 2

School Library Media Budget History

The history of school library media programs is closely tied to the history of school library media funding. Knowing how school libraries were established, and knowing how funding streams began, changed, and slowed, will guide today's budget development processes. Although most agree that the Elementary and Secondary Education Act (ESEA) funding of the 1960s and 1970s accelerated the development of school libraries, library media centers had gained a foothold in most states well before then. The early pioneers of school libraries worked to coax, to cajole, and to demand funding from school district administrators and state legislators. It worked, but not nearly with the same impact as massive federal funding in the 1960s.

Pre-History—Before 1960

The perception of school library media as an acceptable field within the library profession took a huge step forward in 1900, when the first graduate from a professional library school was hired as school librarian for Erasmus High School in New York City. This opened the way for the birth of the idea that the school library was more than a collection of books that was tended to by well-meaning but untrained staffers;

rather, the school library's maintenance was a professional endeavor requiring specialized training (Gillespie & Spirt, 1983, p. 4). Melvil Dewey, a strong supporter of school libraries, was given the credit for this "first," however, the history goes back much further. Even in the Dutch colony of New York, some of the colonial schools had libraries. In North Carolina and some other states, some school libraries existed in high schools before 1900.

In today's school libraries, most allocated funding comes in the form of dollars per pupil. The larger the school, and therefore, the larger the enrollment, the more money the library program receives. However, most of the early attempts to fund school libraries came in the form of matching grants. If the local school district budgeted a certain amount of funds, then the state would match it with equal funds.

In 1901 in North Carolina, the state superintendent put $2,500 in the state budget to be matched in $10 increments by local school districts (Bomar, 1992). In Virginia in the 1930s, the same type of funding was available. Under Charles W. Dickinson, Jr., state supervisor of school libraries, if a local school librarian was able to raise $15.00, then the school district had to match it, and the state of Virginia matched that. Therefore, for every $15.00 raised locally, $60.00 worth of books could be purchased for the school library (Gaver, 1988).

Through this use of matching funds, school libraries could be built according to the desire of the school district to have a school library. The matching funds formula meant that the quality of the library depended on how much the district was willing to spend. The wealth of the school district was not an issue in deciding the quality of the school library and neither was the size of the district or school. Mary Virginia Gaver traveled throughout the south investigating school libraries for her master's thesis in the 1930s. She wrote, "[I] am amazed at the amount of money spent by some country schools on libraries and the backwardness of the wealthy town of Winston-Salem in providing books for its RJ Reynolds Senior High School" (Gaver, 1988).

Matching funds allowed small schools with low enrollment to increase the amount spent on school libraries in a way that per pupil allotments could never do. Although as a funding formula for tax dollars, it has all but disappeared, we are seeing this concept reappear occasionally in grant proposals.

Matching funds tended to disappear from widespread use by the mid-1950s. One aspect of the matching-grant concept that remained for several decades, however, was the state list. Nearly every state maintained a list of "appropriate" books that could be purchased with taxpayer funds. The discount was very large for most of these, but in some states, the titles were narrowly chosen. Gaver noted that publishers and distributors dealing in Virginia were disgruntled with Dickinson's insistence on a large discount. However, the discount only applied to books purchased from the state list. In Montgomery, Alabama, Gaver noticed that in her travels "Sidney Lanier High School has fairly adequate space, but many are duplicates of titles (on account of restricted parallel reading lists)" (Gaver, 1988).

The growth of school libraries in the south was aided in 1913 by the addition of criteria for school libraries in the accreditation standards of the Southern Association of Colleges and Schools (SACS). Still, progress was slow. In 1926, there were only four trained school librarians in the state of North Carolina. The federal role in education was almost nonexistent at this point in terms of providing money for collections, although Work Projects Administration (WPA) projects during the 1930s included the building of school libraries and the renovation of existing schools to include libraries. This effort forestalled the argument of superintendents that there was no room to put the library in a school. As state supervisor of school libraries, Cora Paul Bomar traveled the state to dare superintendents to show her a school in which a library could not be placed (Dickinson, 1987).

As more and more school librarians were hired, and more school districts included rooms for libraries in at least the high schools, concern about the condition of school libraries arose. The link between the school library and student achievement began to draw attention as well. In 1959, a study by the U.S. Office of Education conducted by Rutgers University found that students in schools with school libraries had higher gains on achievement tests than students without school libraries (Gaver, 1963). Through the American Association of School Librarians and the American Library Association, the needs of school libraries began to be discussed at the national level. Strong leaders at the state, the university, and the district levels began to meet to talk about school libraries and the need for every child to have access to a library in the school.

Something else happened about this time that would have an even greater impact on the number and the condition of school libraries and would usher in the "golden age" of school libraries. Sputnik was launched.

The 1960s and the Early 1970s

In 1958, less than half of all schools had libraries, and only 34% of all elementary schools had school libraries. By 1974, that figure had risen to 81% for elementary schools and 85% for high schools. By 1985, the figure had risen to 92% and 93% for elementary and secondary, respectively (Calahan & Hernandez, 1987). Clearly, this was a time of great improvement in school-library service.

With the Russian launch of Sputnik, the legislature of the United States began to talk for the first time about the federal role in the educational process. Education is not mentioned in the Constitution, and therefore, is left to the power of the individual states. Although the need for improved math and science education gave many in Congress a reason for federal intervention, others at the federal level were reluctant to enter an area clearly reserved for state-level authority.

Even when past that hurdle, issues of church and state and of racial segregation prolonged the discussion, especially in terms of educational resources. Congress could simply not agree on race issues, and it also could not decide on whether aid granted to public schools should be available for parochial schools. Historically, there was great inequity in the segregated schools in the south. Mary Gaver wrote that in 1937, eight white schools located in a city in Virginia received $2,374 to buy books for their school libraries, while the total sum for all the segregated schools was $150 (Gaver, 1988).

As these discussions continued in Congress, strong leaders in the school library field began to discuss quietly the impact of potential federal money. Worried, John Rowell, state supervisor of school libraries in Pennsylvania, met with Mary Gaver at Rutgers and noted that there were counties in Pennsylvania where there were "more bears than books" (Gaver, 1988, p. 138). He also was certain that the training and the qualifications of some Pennsylvania school librarians had not prepared them for spending the amount of money that would be possible through this federal funding. This was true in most other states as well. Few school librarians across the country had any library training, and even fewer had gone on to graduate work in library science.

One interesting sidelight of this federal drama was the Ford Fantasy Project, a name coined by Frances Henne, Virginia Mathews, and Mary Virginia Gaver. These three school library pioneers first met in May 1956 to brainstorm what needed to be done if they had the money to do it. The fanciful name came from the need to find a large grant foundation, similar to the Ford Foundation, to take on this project. Interestingly, it was not the Ford Foundation, but rather the Knapp Foundation of North Carolina, that ultimately funded the ideas.

The Knapp Model School Library Project funded eight demonstration school libraries across the country. Five of these schools were elementary, and one was a segregated school in Baltimore. Thousands of school librarians visited these schools to educate themselves on the modern, 1960s concept of a school library.

Resources were not the only concern of the Knapp initiatives. The three-phase School Library Manpower Project was also funded by the Knapp Foundation. Phase one of this project was to identify the tasks performed by school librarians. The published result of this phase was the Behavioral Requirements Analysis Checklist (BRAC) (Case & Lowrey, 1973). BRAC divides the work of the school library media specialist into seven major areas of competence (Human Behavior, Learning and Learning Environment, Planning and Evaluation, Media, Management, Research, and Professionalism). Under each area, functions are listed in behavioral terms, with individual tasks under each function.

Although worded in 1960s terminology, BRAC areas of competence, functions, and tasks still ring true today. School library media specialists will recognize tasks such as working with teachers to instruct students in information skills, building a collection based on student interest, and encouraging reading along with the other program management aspects of the school library media center. Figure 2.1 lists some of the BRAC functions focused on budgeting processes.

> **Figure 2.1:** Behavioral Requirements Analysis Checklist Excerpted Tasks

> ## Functions Related to Budgeting Behavioral Requirements Analysis Checklist
>
> **C. Planning and Evaluation**
> Function 6: To design, develop, and write proposals for the acquisition of local, state, and federal funds to support and extend the media program.
>
> 10 tasks listed
>
> ---
>
> **D. Media**
> Function 5: To acquire media and equipment for the media center program.
>
> 16 tasks listed
>
> ---
>
> **E. Management**
> Function 9: To prepare and justify the media program budget for the implementation of the media program.
>
> 14 tasks listed
>
> Function 10: To administer the media program budget for the implementation of the media program.
>
> 13 tasks listed
>
> Function 11: To prepare and administer the budget for media center resources and equipment as a part of special projects funded by private, local, state, or federal monies.
>
> 5 tasks listed

The BRAC list of almost 700 tasks performed by school librarians was used as the basis for phase two of the Knapp Project, which was to support model performance-based school library media education programs. Originally, the Knapp Project was designed with only two phases. However, near the end of phase two, it became apparent that the lack of an assessment phase to survey school librarians who had completed the model programs and who were now practicing school librarians was necessary.

Also during this time, Congress resolved the church and state issue by allowing public schools to loan materials and textbooks to parochial schools. This decision paved the way for the Elementary and Secondary Education Act (ESEA) in 1965. President Johnson signed this bill into law and began the authorization for school library resources under Title II of this act at $100 million. The flow of this money greatly accelerated the establishment of school libraries. This money was not only used for books. Introduction of audiovisual materials began to change traditional school libraries into school library media centers, and to cause school librarians to evolve into school library media specialists. This change may not have been as successful without the infusion of such large amounts of ready money.

Although ESEA funding continued throughout the Sixties and into the early 1970s, pressure began almost immediately after the first year to reduce funding. Very few years saw the full entitlement reflected in the budget. Funding never rose higher than $105 million for this program, and, at its lowest point, was reduced to $50 million in 1969 under the pressure of Vietnam War efforts.

The American Library Association, the National Educational Association, and other groups formed an emergency funding committee, which later became the Committee for Full Funding of Education Programs. This committee, the first sustained, joint lobbying effort focused on school libraries, was successful in convincing Congress to maintain funding at close to the original appropriation. Frase, noting the success of this group, said that although there were fluctuations in the economy, changing attitudes of members of Congress, and changing presidential administrations, the pressure of the committee was the constant factor that preserved this funding for as long as it did (Frase, 1974). Figure 2.2 illustrates the work of this committee.

Figure 2.2: Committee for Full Funding

Impact of the Committee for Full Funding School Library Media Resources

	Included in Budget		Eventual Monies Spent
FY 1969	$46,000,000		$ 50,000,000
FY 1970	0		42,500,000
FY 1971	80,000,000		80,000,000
FY 1972	80,000,000		90,000,000
FY 1973	90,000,000		100,000,000
FY 1974	0		90,200,000

From data in Frase, 1974.

The success of the Committee for Full Funding was truly phenomenal. As can be seen in Figure 2.2, even without the support of the presidential administration, this committee preserved the funding for library programs at a level that was at or above the original appropriation. When President Lyndon Johnson left office, his 1970 budget contained the same appropriation as in 1969. President Richard Nixon made general reductions of 10% or more in all government programs. Library programs in general received a 66% cut, but for school libraries, the amount appropriated was zero. Again, the committee began applying pressure, and from 1970—1975, almost $500 million was administered to library programs.

Such an effort, in a reduced economic climate, could not be sustained forever. In addition, because funding was always almost eliminated and then restored at the last minute, sometimes by the overturn of a presidential veto, no long-range or even short-range planning for the optimum use of the funds was possible. School library support services at the district, the regional, and the state levels were always at the brink of extinction and were then pulled back at the last minute to be reinstated for one more year.

An unintended effect of ESEA that has remained to this day to some extent is the effect on local budgets for school library media programs. Because of the sheer amount of money this legislation poured into school libraries, local school district budget allocations for school library media programs were reduced, even with great uncertainty over the continuation of the federal funding. When the federal money eventually all but disappeared, and when the economy took a downturn, school library budgets were left in a state of dramatic decline.

Albeit with some negative aftereffects, the success of this period in school library history is undeniable. Frase notes in his review of funding for this period that "looking back it was clear that the goal was to ensure school libraries of reasonable quality—and that substantial progress was made" (Frase, 1974, p. 7). From the Department of Education survey report, we know that the percentage of schools with school libraries rose from 50% in 1958 to 93% in 1985 (Calahan & Hernandez, 1987). However, it is also true that ESEA also created a reliance on a money stream flowing from beyond the parameters of the school district budget directly to the door of the school library. Because of the sheer size of this money flow, school districts were able to reduce funding for the school libraries. When the federal funding was eliminated, there were little to no other funds available.

This elimination of federal funding came at a time when the economic climate was not encouraging. For school boards that had reduced funding because of the large amount of federal funds, the idea of allocating new money to library programs was simply not something they perceived as fiscally responsible. Federal funding had lasted long enough and turnover of school boards and school administrators recent enough that memories of the responsibility of a school district to fund school libraries either did not exist or was diminished. As the library program was built with federal funds, the library became another federal program that would not exist without continued federal funding.

The establishment of school library media programs and resources was the strength of categorical federal funding for school libraries, and the library community has never ceased efforts to replace it. Categorical funding is created by the federal government in order to meet specific national objectives; in this case, the establishment and the maintenance of school libraries are the objectives. Once a goal was substantially completed, categorical funding was collapsed into block grants that could be spent either on school libraries or on other areas. School districts were given great flexibility over how these funds were spent. Choices were made in most cases to distribute the money from the block grants to a variety of local needs, such as providing guidance services, establishing reading initiatives, and other areas that, although valuable to the educational process, further reduced the amounts the school library media specialists had to spend.

Categorical funds not only provided money for materials, but the resulting collections encouraged schools to find rooms in the schools to be set up as libraries and to hire certified school librarians to manage those collections and library services. The money also increased district and state level support services for school library media programs. ESEA Title II funds also made it possible for school libraries to evolve into media centers, with audiovisual materials and equipment becoming part of the then-modern school library.

In 2002, ESEA funding for school library media programs is again becoming a reality. We must not become dependent on the federal money stream as we did before, and we cannot afford to allow federal funds to replace school district budget allocations. Constant vigilance is needed to remind the school district administration of the ebb of the funding tide that created the modern school library with 30-year-old collections, many with "ESEA" still stamped inside the covers.

Post-1975

With the implementation of block grants, school districts still had the option to use allowable funds for school libraries; yet few districts made that choice. Paul Simon reported that "In 1966 ... Congress appropriated the equivalent of $536 million (in 1995 dollars). In 1992, school library media centers received only $104 million." According to figures presented in Chapter 2 of Simon's book, only 29% of allowable funds went to school libraries in 1992 (Simon, 1995).

For the most part, school libraries remained strong, at least in terms of program and mission if not in collections and resources. The literature in the mid-1980s reveals the struggle, however. In some states, the closings of school libraries were reported, and budgets remained only a fraction of what they were in 1965. Figure 2.3 illustrates the dire status of libraries in some states with a list of citations from some professional journals of the period.

> **Figure 2.3:** Sampling of 1980s Literature
>
> # Articles
>
> Adcock, D.S. *Closing—School Library Media Centers.* Ilinois Libraries 66: 92-4, February 1984.
>
> Baldridge, Sherie W. and Marsha D. Broadway. *Who Needs an Elementary School Librarian?* Principal 67(2): 37-40. November 1987.
>
> Bobinski, M.F. *Survival of Public Libraries.* New York Library Association Bulletin 28: 1+, May 1980.
>
> California. *City Librarians Protest School Library Cuts.* School Library Journal vol. 31: 8+, January 1985.
>
> from Pub. Admin. Series: Bibliography #P 2813

It is important to note that federal, non-categorical, and indirect aid to school libraries remained strong, although this assistance has been mostly overlooked as an aid source. Assistance in cataloging by the Library of Congress continued and grew in popularity. Statistical surveys on the quality of school libraries were conducted in 1974, 1978, and again in 1985 by the Department of Education (an office within the cabinet of the Department of Health, Education, and Welfare). Assistance continued to other types of libraries that still provided some benefits, although indirectly, for school libraries, such as interlibrary loan assistance to public libraries.

It is also important to note that even though ESEA included funds mostly for materials, it had an impact on other areas of the library budget. Because staff was needed to manage the materials, the positions of school library media specialist and library media assistant or clerk were established in most schools, and in a few fortunate states, were written into state mandates. The position of library supervisor was created in many districts to handle the acquisition, the organization, and the paperwork load of the federal funds. Although in some states, while the mandated, building-level positions have remained, the positions at the district, the regional, and the state levels have not fared so well. Many regional and district-level library media supervisors were dismissed, were reassigned, or had their positions eliminated upon retirement. At the state level, other responsibilities were folded into the library media role over time.

Frase (1974) notes that the federal fiscal policy in the 1980s was affected by four factors. First, the National Council on Library and Information Sciences advocated renewal of aid to libraries for two more years, which may have been seen as a death knell for continued funding. Second, the first White House Conference on

Libraries focused on programs rather than resources. Third, there was the turndown in the economy, which was beyond anyone's direct control. And lastly, the emphasis on tax cuts and on continuing the previous administration's focus on collapsing categorical aid into block grants probably had the greatest effect. The reauthorization of ESEA contained aid for school libraries, as well as guidance and counseling, along with other materials and equipment not necessarily intended for school libraries. As was noted before, although school district administrators could make the choice to continue to fund school library programs, the reduced amount of money and the new choices available for the uses of funds made it unlikely that programs could continue with the same strength as before.

Historical Data and Statistics

There have been two major series of data with regards to school library media program expenditures and resources. The Department of Education (DOE), formerly part of the Department of Health, Education, and Welfare, conducted surveys in 1958, 1960, 1962, 1974, 1978, and 1985. Also considered part of the DOE surveys, the massive School and Staffing Survey (SASS) included information regarding school library media programs and resources for the first time in 1995. Since the early 1980, School Library Journal (SLJ) has published the results of a mostly biennial survey, conducted by Marilyn Miller, first in conjunction with Barbara Moran and later with Marilyn Shontz (Miller & Moran, 1983).

These two data series can be combined to provide a more complete look at the funding picture. The reported findings from each year of the data series are included in the Figure 2.4 and Figure 2.5. The authority for combining the two series of data comes from Calahan's report on the 1985 DOE survey. In her review, she included a statistical comparison of the past DOE surveys with the SLJ surveys and found that they could be viewed congruently, although the surveys had different goals and sampled different sets of participants.

The data in Figure 2.4 and Figure 2.5 reflect what we already know from the literature. When the federal funding ended, materials could not be replaced and, therefore, tended to remain on the shelves. Callahan and Hernandez (1987) noted the statistic that the mean book collections increased from 2,972 volumes in 1958 to 8,466 volumes in 1985. Most school library media specialists know that this statistic is more likely a function of "what was purchased, stayed," than an indication of quality. Figure 2.4 shows the rise in the mean collection size from pre-ESEA days until the present. The years given for the surveys, 1958—2000, were the years as reported. Some of the data was reported in academic years (1982—1983). Other data was reported as a single year (1985).

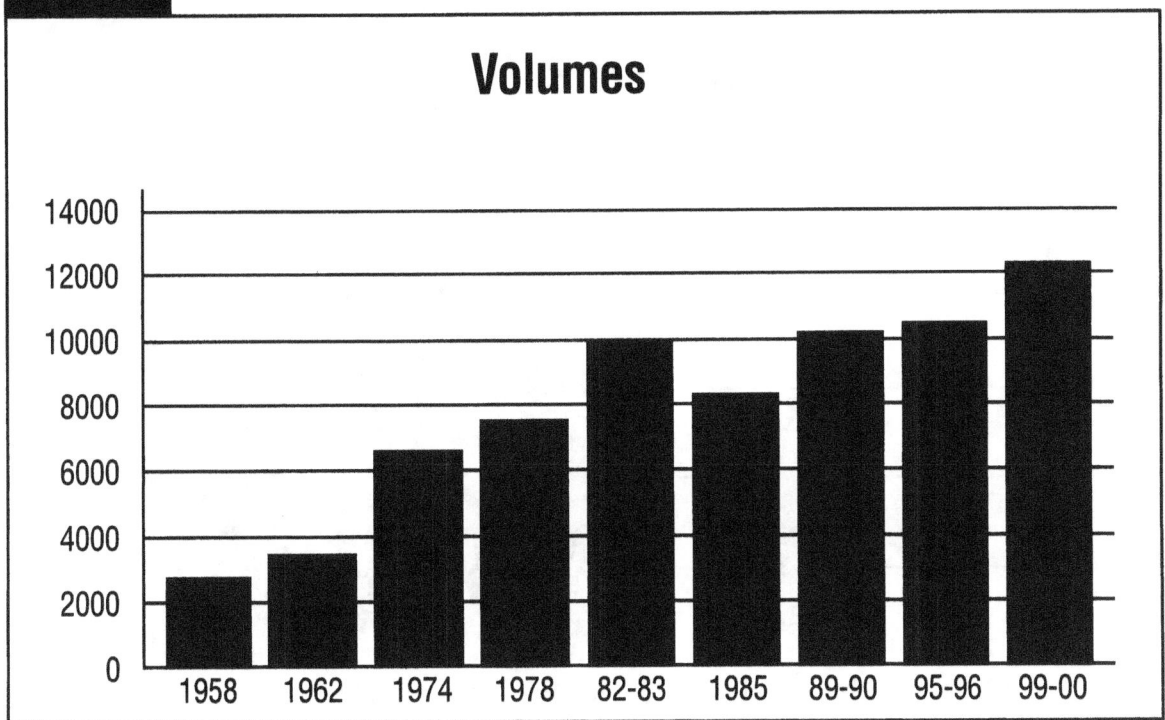

Figure 2.4: Mean Collection Size, 1958-2000

From Figure 2.4, we see an overall and rather steady rise in the total number of volumes in library collections, with the exception of the slight dip in 1985. However, it must also be noted that during the time period shown in Figure 2.4, the size of schools steadily increased as well. Remember also that by the late 1950s, funding streams were usually based on per pupil allotment instead of matching funds. In order to look truly at the growth of collections, volumes purchased per pupil is probably more accurate.

Figure 2.5 shows the mean number of books held per pupil over the same time period given in Figure 2.4 (1958—2000) and is more telling. From this graph we can see that size relative to student population is staying the same. This is probably not a good thing, since without funds to purchase new books, older books are simply staying on the shelves. On paper, it looks as if the library media program is continuing to meet the needs of students. In reality, however, the changing needs of students cannot be met with stagnating collections.

Figure 2.5: Mean Collection per Pupil, 1958-2000

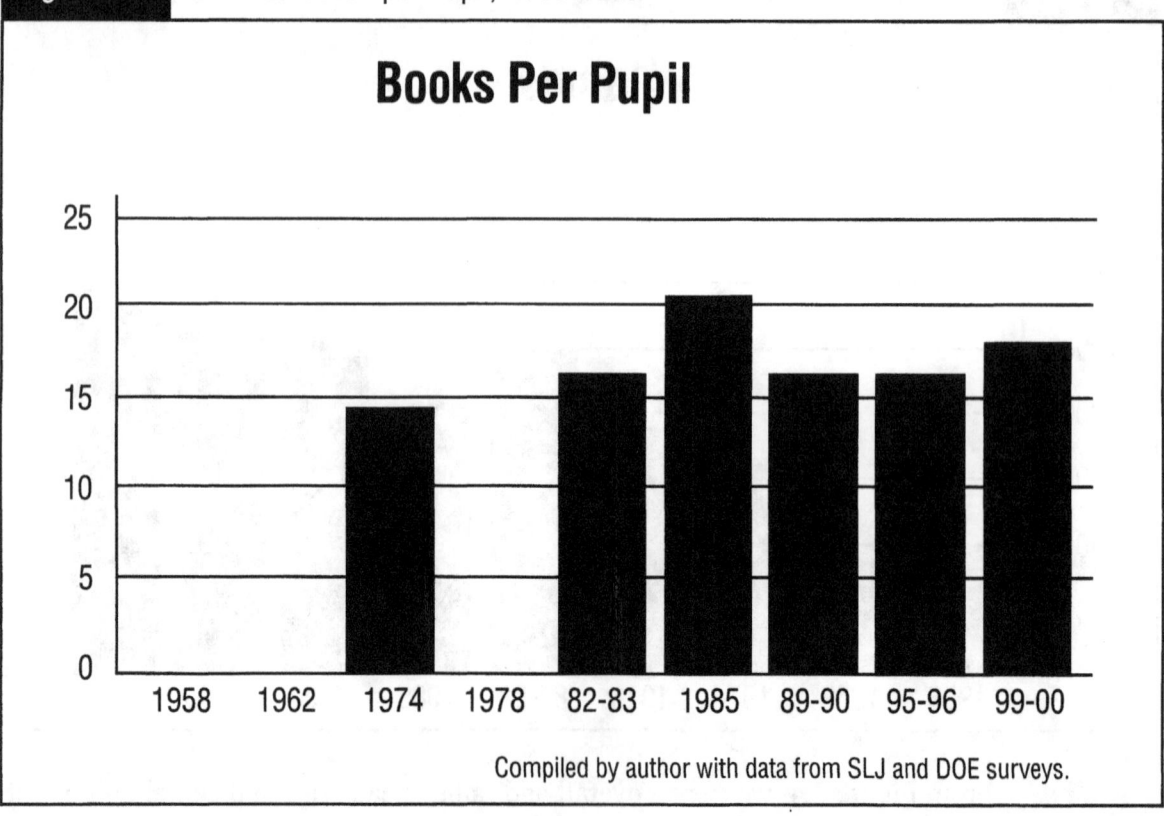

Compiled by author with data from SLJ and DOE surveys.

Furthermore, there is also concern with the unknown statistics regarding the relationship of school size to collection size. Any increase in school size does not necessarily have a proportional increase in collection size. More work has to be done to analyze a prototype of excellence in school library media collections. Until we can present a working model of excellence, it is difficult to discuss with precision the needs of the students in a school relative to the size and quality of the book collection.

The growth of information technology began to impact school library collections in the early Eighties. School librarians still bought books for the library shelves, but they were also buying filmstrips, microforms, films—and later still—videotapes, CD-ROMs and computer software. The technology required to support a library book is essentially a shelf. To support the new types of information technology, many thousands of dollars have been spent for computers and other equipment.

Automation is another factor that may have affected library book budgets. The typical answer found in the research literature to, "How much money does it cost to automate?" was usually, as Porter put it, "more than you expect" (Porter, 1991, p. 90). The amount of money required to convert print catalogs, to purchase equipment, and to wire libraries for automation and networked resources is a continuing expense. Although there has been speculation that automation and information technology expenditures have had a negative impact on the school library budget, we will see from later graphs and statistics in this chapter that expenditures for library books may not have been as negatively affected as originally thought. More research will need to be done on exactly where the money came from to automate libraries.

Site-based management (SBM) has also affected the school library media program and the school library media budget. In the waves of school reform that swept through education beginning in the early 1980s, decision-making authority in the school district was decentralized to the school level (Verstegen, 1994). In many districts, teams of teachers, parents, and other school personnel were given the authority to decide issues previously left to the principal's discretion. Allocation of available funds within the school was sometimes part of the site-based management team's responsibility. In the early 1990s, both Betty Hamilton (Hamilton, 1993) and Daniel Barron (Barron, 1992) discussed ways that school library media specialists could work with the site-based management team. Many suggestions focused on the potential power of becoming a SBM team member or even a chairperson; this was a responsibility many school library media specialists chose in order to keep the money necessary to have the library programs active and functioning.

More research has to be done to review the impact of school site-based management teams on library media programs. One decision-making task sometimes handed to site-based management teams is the authority, at least on a limited basis, to determine budget allocations within the school. This caused much consternation for school library media specialists who concentrated on relationships with their building principals to secure their budget allocations and who then found the decision was given to a group of classroom teachers with differing levels of interest or support for the school library media program. More about the budget process with site-based decision-making teams and some specific strategies are included in Chapter 3.

Statistical Procedure

In order to truly learn the impact of federal funding, it is necessary to have an overview of the budget figures over the last several decades. This is achieved by a mathematical equation to bring the amount budgeted for a particular year up to the most current year for which statistics are available. At the end of this chapter, the formula is explained in more detail. In statistical terms, *original dollars* refer to the amount budgeted, for instance, $1.85 in 1958. *Current dollars* refer to that same amount, calculated to what it would be in 2000.

One note of caution is needed before reviewing these statistics. Although statistics were regularly reported, they were reported in varying ways. For instance, the "things" in the data survey were counted differently each year that DOE surveys were conducted. Even the meaning of "per pupil" changed. In some years, the number of pupils in a particular school was used to calculate per pupil expenditures. In other years, pupils and dollars from the entire state were added to make an overall total and were then calculated. Although this makes just a slight difference in the resulting calculation, it is an example of the differences that call these statistics into question.

All statistics are usually slightly inaccurate, and the best authorities will agree that you use the best available statistics that you have. The charts and tables included in this book may be little more than a best guess at times, but it is important to take into consideration any information to give insight into the history of school library media program funding. The best supporting explanation for using this data is that although it can be argued that this data are flawed, it is the best representation we have of what happened with funding over time. A fuzzy, out-of-focus picture can be considered better than no picture at all.

Library Media Book Expenditures

What has happened to expenditures of library books over time? Figure 2.6 shows the reported expenditure for library books since the first survey in 1958. The column entitled "Mean per pupil library media expenditure" refers to original dollars, or the actual dollar figure reported for that year. The "Current dollar mean book expenditure" column shows the same figure once it has been brought to 1999—2000 equivalent value.

Figure 2.6: Historical Overview of School Library Media Book Expenditures

Year	Mean per pupil library book expenditure	Current dollar mean book expenditure
58-59	1.6	9.22
62-63	2.28	12.58
74-75	4.22	14.26
78-79	4.25	10.86
82-83	4.58	7.91
83-84	5.48	9.17
85-86	6.01	9.31
88-89	6.95	9.79
89-90	8.09	10.87
91-92	8.38	10.25
93-94	8.9	10.26
95-96	8.54	9.34
97-98	10.88	11.29
99-00	11.41	11.41

Compiled by author with data from SLJ and DOE surveys.

With the data from Figure 2.6, it is clear that federal funding had a tremendous impact, both in the creation of funding for school library media resources and in the decline of funding as well. Apart from the slight increase in the late 1980s, and another slight increase in the last several years, the field basically has not gained much ground since 1958. The amount spent per pupil for library books in 1995 was only $0.12 more per pupil than in 1958. Even with the increase in the last reported year, dollars per pupil are still less than the 1962 level.

Another way to look at this data is to compare the dollars spent per pupil with the reported price of a youth library book. Figure 2.7 illustrates this; it shows the number of books that were purchased per pupil during given school years.

Figure 2.7: Books Purchased Per Pupil

Year	Number of books purchased per pupil
58-59	0.64
62-63	0.82
74-75	0.84
78-79	0.64
82-83	0.52
83-84	0.56
85-86	0.49
88-89	0.53
89-90	0.61
91-92	0.59
93-94	0.60
95-96	0.56
97-98	0.70

Compiled by author with data from SLJ and DOE surveys.

In the 1960 standards, the goal of one new book per student per year was introduced. Although we may say that this is an unreachable target and will be never achieved, the 1960 standards gave this figure as a minimum (AASL, 1960, p. 83). As seen by Figure 2.7, that goal was never achieved, even in the strongest budget years. The closest that U.S. school libraries came to that statistic was in the 1960s and early 1970s, with a high of .84 books per pupil reported in 1974. In contrast, less than half a book per pupil was purchased in the mid-1980s.

The impact of these statistics on the conditions of school library book collections is all too real for library media specialists. The sheer numbers of books that were purchased in the decade of federal funding built collections is daunting. These books, because of the sharp decline in allocations in the late 1970s and 1980s, have never been able to be replaced. In many schools, these books may still be the backbone of the collection.

Other Materials

What about other resources in the collection? A look at the numbers in Figure 2.8 reveals some interesting trends regarding the per pupil expenditures for materials other than books at the elementary level, using the data from the School Library Journal (SLJ) surveys.

Figure 2.8: Trend Analysis of Non-Book Resources (Elementary)

	Elementary Level			
Years	Periodicals	AV	Software	CD-ROM
83-84	1.68	4.59		
85-86	1.55	4.55	0.25	
89-90	1.70	4.37	1.71	
91-92	1.57	3.03	2.3	1.65
93-94	1.52	3.88	2.04	1.1
95-96	1.42	2.17	3.03	1.27
97-98	1.54	2.53	2.42	1.35
Difference	-0.12	-2.06	2.42	1.35

Compiled by author with data from SLJ surveys.

The SLJ surveys are extremely useful in reviewing the impact of new technologies on school library media budgets. Note, according to Figure 2.8, during the 1982—1983 school year, new technologies were just beginning to make an impact on school library media budgets. Using these surveys over time, we can see the impact of new technologies over time. With elementary schools, for example, the low of just $0.25 per pupil for computer software in 1985 indicates that this could be considered the beginning year for such an expenditure. It is clear that the decline in the purchase of audiovisual resources coincided with the increase in software and CD-ROMs. Periodicals stayed roughly the same. Audiovisual resources decreased by 2.06%, while at the same time, software increased by 2.42%.

Compare those figures with the trend analysis of high school non-book resources, shown in Figure 2.9.

Figure 2.9: Trend Analysis of Non-Book Resources (High School)

High School Level

Years	Periodicals	AV	Software	CD-ROM
83-84	3.66	5.22		
85-86	3.80	4.94	0.09	
89-90	3.84	3.66	1.28	
91-92	4.08	2.63	2.23	2.51
93-94	4.08	3.25	1.85	3.53
95-96	3.50	2.15	2.65	4.11
97-98	3.46	2.05	3.10	3.40
Difference	-0.20	-3.17	3.1	3.40

Compiled by author with data from SLJ surveys.

A complete list of the SLJ issues in which the survey results appeared is included in the bibliography. Careful reading of these issues can provide fascinating data that school library media specialists can use to gain insight into the implementation of new technologies in school library media programs.

These surveys, conducted by Marilyn Miller with Barbara Moran and later with Marilyn Shontz, provide a clear picture of the budget statistics by category and can be extremely useful. However, what these charts do not tell us is why the amounts increased or declined. We may know that periodicals declined by 12% in elementary schools and by 20% in high school, but we don't know what that means. Are school library media specialists spending more on electronic, full-text periodical sources and thereby decreasing their periodical budgets to avoid duplication? Or are they deliberately decreasing the number of periodicals received to preserve the library book budget? We don't know the answers to these very important questions surrounding the decisions that were made by school library media specialists regarding how to spend the limited funds that they were being granted in order to meet the resource needs of students and staff.

We can speculate as to the decline in audiovisual resources. Where school library media collections once contained expensive 16mm films, filmstrips, film loops, and a variety of other media, now school library media specialists are purchasing fewer varieties of media for their collections at a much cheaper cost. This decline is to be expected and almost matches the amount spent on computer software. With future research, it may be possible to say that electronic information resources in libraries did not impact the library book budget, but rather the audiovisual materials budget, and may be a natural and expected outcome of format changes over time. However, that research has not yet been conducted.

Summary

What do we know from the past about funding for school library media programs? First, we know that strong people with vision made an incredible impact on the creation of school library media centers. We know also that school libraries had a foothold in many schools long before ESEA, largely as a result of school librarians with determination and a belief in the need for all children to have access to libraries.

We also know that it wasn't easy. While we might look back and think of all that money pouring into school libraries, we also have to remember that the Committee for Full Funding had to fight for every dime. Before that, strong state leadership strategized and lobbied for improvement in school libraries.

The U.S Constitution does not mention education, therefore, it is a power reserved to the states. Historically, the federal role in education has been limited, and the federal government has been reluctant to create unfunded mandates that would interfere in the sovereignty of the states. The federal role has typically been that of a junior partner, concentrating on equity issues, such as school lunch, special and remedial education, and protection against discrimination, rather than on programs that are more central to the type and level of instruction offered in the entire school.

At this writing, we have just achieved federal funding again for school libraries. Will that funding, so long awaited, be in danger as continuously as it was before in the earlier cycle? And if that is true, will there be a committee to lobby for continued funding and renewal? Will increases in federal spending mean substantial decreases in local school district allocations? Time will tell.

It is important to know how your budget stacks up against the budget statistics from the past. As noted previously in this chapter, in a school with 10,000 books and 1,000 pupils, a collection should have been completed replaced three times since 1958. Are you ahead or behind that statistic? Here's how to tell.

STEP 1: DIG!

Find out how much money was spent in the past for school libraries in your district. Go back through old files, look for old reports, call the central office, and ask what statistics are available. Friendliness with the office clerical staff can be very helpful. Many times a school secretary can put her hands on data that no one else knows exists.

In years past, an end-of-the-year report on collections and finances was required from each school library. Find all the reports from as far back as you can.

Remember, though, that columns of numbers will glaze the most avid supporter. Choose several years for comparison, either the years used in this chapter, or an every five-year or three-year comparison. You also will need to find the school enrollment for each year in order to do the dollars per pupil comparison.

Record the data carefully for transfer into a spreadsheet. Figure 2.10 shows a sample data record sheet for library books.

Figure 2.10: Spreadsheet Worksheet

Year	School Enrollment	Amount Spent for Books	Number of Books Purchased per Pupil

STEP 2: MATH!

Complete the calculation in Figure 2.10 to determine the dollars per pupil spent for books in a given year.

Look ahead to Figure 2.11. The result of the calculation from Figure 2.10—dividing the amount spent for books by the school enrollment—will be the "Original Dollars" column for the spreadsheet in Figure 2.11. The steps in the next paragraph outline the calculation to bring the original dollars up to current dollars.

There are two easy ways to bring the money up to the current year for comparison. One is a matter of a few clicks on the Bureau of Labor Statistics (BLS) Web site, the other involves math, and perhaps a spreadsheet. Which one is easiest depends on how much data you have. If you have decided to start with library books going back every five years since 1980, it is probably easiest to use the BLS Web site. However, columns of data are easier to decipher using the spreadsheet method.

Regardless of which method you choose, you need to prepare your data. Title the column with the actual money that was reported "Original Dollars." Title the column that will contain the dollars as of the current year "Current Dollars."

Doing the Math

The math steps below may seem complicated at first. Work through each calculation, double-checking with the BLS Web site. Once you understand the process, you will find it extremely useful.

In order to bring up the original dollars to current dollars, you will need the average Consumer Price Index (CPI) index for each year for which you have data. This can be found at <ftp://ftp.bls.gov/pub/special.requests/cpi/cpiai.txt>. However, that site changes frequently. The table you are looking for is the "Annual Percent Increase Since 1913." To find it, go to the Bureau of Labor Statistics Web site at <http://www.bls.gov>. Under "Inflation and Consumer Spending," click on "Consumer Price Index." Scroll down and click on "Tables Created by BLS," then on "Annual Percent Increase Since 1913." Although the Web site may change over time, these areas should still be available somewhere.

You will now be looking at monthly CPI index figures by year, starting with 1913, which is the first year for which the CPI was calculated. Scroll over to the right, and you will see the average for that year. Although it would be interesting to see the difference in funds allocated for the library in 1913 and the funds allocated at the present time, very few schools have preserved that data. Scroll down and note the average CPI for each year for which you have data. Make a column in your spreadsheet for these numbers. Your spreadsheet should now look like Figure 2.11.

Figure 2.11: Spreadsheet Worksheet (Revised)

Year	School Enrollment	Amount Spent for Books per Pupil	CPI Index	Amount Spent for Books per Pupil
		Original Dollars		*Current Dollars*

Decide what year will be the Current Dollars. This is usually the last year for which you have data. In the example shown in Figure 2.12, the current year is 2000. The average CPI for that year, according to the chart on the BLS Web site, is 172.21. That number will be used in each calculation.

Figure 2.12: Current Dollar Calculation

Formula: (Current Year CPI * Original Dollars) / Original CPI

Calculation: (172.2 * $10) / 124 = $13.89.

The formula for bringing original dollars to current dollars requires multiplying the original dollars by the CPI of the current year and then dividing by the CPI of the original dollar year.

For instance, suppose that you found that $10 per pupil was spent on the library program in 1989. That figure increased to $12 per pupil in the 2000—2001 school year. Although that is an increase, you suspect that the buying power of your budget has declined. You would like to prove that overall your buying power has decreased, not increased. To show that, you need to know what $10 in 1989 is worth today. Review the elements of the formula.

*Formula: (Current Year CPI * Original Dollars) / Original CPI*

In English, that can be translated to say that the Consumer Price Index of the last year for which you have data is multiplied by the year for which you have original dollars, and then, that figure is divided by the average Consumer Price Index for the original dollar year.

After checking the BLS Web site, you see that the CPI for 2000 is 172.2. The average CPI for 1989 is 124. The calculation below shows the formula with those numbers added.

*Calculation: (172.2 * $10) / 124 = $13.89.*

The spreadsheet in Figure 2.13 shows that calculation completed for the comparison years as well as the result. As suspected, there has been a steady decline in the library budget, even though the allocation has increased.

Figure 2.13: Completed Spreadsheet

Year	Amount Spent for Books per Pupil	CPI Index	Amount Spent for Books per Pupil
	Original Dollars	Formula = (Current Year CPI * Original Dollars) / Original CPI	Current Dollars Formula = (Current Year CPI * Original Dollars) / Original CPI
1989-90	$10.00	124	$13.89
1994-95	$11.00	148.2	$12.78
2000-01	$12.00	172.2	$12.00

If these figures matched the data from your research into the budget allocation history in your school, you could say that in order to keep the same allocation that you had in 1989, the dollars per pupil in 2000 should have been $13.89. Since your enrollment may have changed as well, this can be an extremely powerful bargaining tool. Even if your enrollment has remained stable, for a school of 500 students, the decline of over $500 per year for over 10 years has had a tremendous negative effect on the ability of the library media program to serve the needs of students and teachers.

This data can be taken further by using the average price of a library book. Find this data for your school by dividing the amount spent for library books by the number of books purchased. Conventional wisdom says that this figure is around $15.00. If your data is typical to that presented in Figure 2.13, in a school with 500 pupils, your ability to update the collection has been reduced by around 63 books a year ($1.89, which is the difference in the budget over time, times the number of pupils in the school (500), divided by the average price per book). It is easy to see the amount of damage done over time by limited budgets. This method can also be used to show the impact of limited budget increases on other materials formats as well.

No Math Required

Although the no math required technique may seem easier, if you have columns of numbers, a spreadsheet can quickly do these calculations once you have the numbers in the spreadsheet cells. However, for some people, not doing the calculation will always be preferred.

On the Bureau of Labor Statistics Web site, click on "Inflation Calculator." A little window pops up and asks you to fill in the blanks for "$____ in year ____ has the same buying power as (blank) in ____ year." Fill in the data, click "Calculate," and the math is done.

Instructional Opportunity Method

Show your data to one of the math or business teachers. The skills used in this step will be a good review for basic math and spreadsheet skills. The students will have a real-life project to use basic math skills, and you have a great collaborative activity. Finding the CPI numbers on the BLS Web site and showing the impact over time is a great opportunity for integrating math and information skills in a collaborative instructional project. The students can make charts and graphs and may have very creative ways of displaying the data in far more detail and depth than most school library media specialists will have time to do.

In the next chapter, we will get more involved in the use of this data. For now, begin to start gathering, organizing, and calculating. It is sometimes amazing to see how buying power has dramatically decreased over time.

Since you know the national averages in the figures used in this chapter, are you ahead of the national average or behind? If, on a national scale, school libraries are purchasing one library book for every two pupils, how many are you purchasing? What is the effect of being slightly behind over time? This is another great project for a math or a business class. Some students will come up with greater insights, better slogans, and more interesting statistics than anyone else.

At the beginning of this section it was noted that a collection of 10,000 volumes would have be renewed three times since 1958. Has the library program in your school been able to keep up?

What Would Savvy School Library Media Specialists Do?

Savvy school library media specialists don't guess. They know. They've done the action research, and they know the published research of the field. They read professional journals, and they check the research journals of the field for any new insights into their own school library media programs.

Savvy school library media specialists apply for grants, but they make sure that the grants are seen as beyond the normal funding responsibility of the school district. When asked for budget amounts, they do not include book fairs, grants, or other funding. A budget is a stable funding source, not a one-time activity that may or may not be included in the future.

Savvy school library media specialists know their history. They know when their school libraries were built, renovated, or expanded. They know when the program had a lot of money, and when the budget was zero. They can apply that knowledge to show the impact of those times on the library program. Just as the rings on a tree can show times of drought, fire, or rapid growth, so can a library collection through analysis of copyright dates, which can be thought of as show times of feast or famine.

Chapter 3

Understanding Budget Terms and Processes

Abra-ca-da-bra! Although no one really would believe that a magic wand is waved and a budget is produced, few employees of a school district would say that they have any understanding of how money is translated from coins in the taxpayer's wallet to resources on the shelves in a school. In order to maximize efforts to increase the school library media budget allocation by working through school district budget procedures, a basic understanding of school district finance is necessary.

One can learn a lot by watching how a school district spends money. Education is an expensive process, and even the smallest districts may have budgets that are valued into the millions. Very few teaching and learning processes can be automated. Even with the influx of technology into the school, the teacher-student ratio is still a crucial component of a good school. The interaction between the district and the taxpayers' money has two elements: financial policy and fiscal policy. Financial policy is how the district handles and spends its tax revenue. Fiscal policy, on the other hand, is how the district approaches the larger issues of taxation, liberal or conservative spending, and how they approach the budgeting process.

If you are at all familiar with economics, you have likely heard of microeconomics and macroeconomics. In terms of our discussion, the way money is applied to specific situations and events is considered microeconomics. A broad look at the meaning of money issues is considered macroeconomics. In this book, microeconomics, and also the district's fiscal procedures and policies, will be the focus for developing the school district budget. Advocacy, in Chapter 4, strikes more at changing the district's concepts and approaches to spending money on the library media program, i.e., a more macroeconomic approach.

The terminology used to discuss budget processes in the school district is extremely important. Some taxpayers feel education is a business that can be compared to organizations of similar size in the private business sector. Some districts have even considered hiring business-trained people, rather than educators, as superintendents. To appeal to this strong and vocal group, it will help if the correct terminology is used to request funds or to gain input into the budget processes. If nothing else, it helps to portray the school library media program as a fiscally savvy and financially sound investment and the library media specialist as an expert manager of resources and services.

How the Money Gets There

As mentioned before in the previous chapter, education is not mentioned in the U.S. Constitution. Each state, therefore, has the authority and the responsibility to develop an education system according to the state constitution and state regulations. Not surprisingly, the organizational structures that frame schools and school districts vary widely from state to state. Nowhere does education vary so much as in the area of how schools are financed and organized. The number of school districts, the authority of the school districts to decide how much money is needed, and how the money is delivered are all very different from state to state. For instance, the entire state of Hawaii is one school district, while the state of New York has over 700 districts. School district boundaries are sometimes the same as the boundaries of the city or county. Other districts cross municipal boundaries at will. Although there may be even further idiosyncrasies that are state-related, one of the descriptions in the paragraphs that follow most likely fits the definition of your state.

In some states, the school district is a function of county or city government, such as in Florida, North Carolina, or Virginia. In these states, the school district boundaries are the same as the county or city boundaries. The administrative structure of the school district and the school board are under the financial authority of the municipal boundaries. A school district budget, after being passed by the school board, must then be passed by the municipality government before it is enacted. For instance, a county school board passes the school district budget. The budget is then passed to the county government for approval, most likely the county commissioners or whatever that governing body may be named.

However, in other states, New York and Pennsylvania for example, a school district is a government entity in itself and has the power to tax on its own behalf. In these states, a school district may be made up of one high school and its feeder schools, with no attention to county boundaries. There tends to be many more school districts in states using this structure; New York, for instance, with over 700 school districts and Pennsylvania with around 500. Population has little to do with the number of districts; a large city, such as Buffalo or Philadelphia, is just one school district.

In states using a structure that results in many small school districts, there are usually regional entities designed to provide services that would prove too expensive for the small school districts to provide entirely on their own. The Board of Cooperative Educational Services (BOCES) in New York state is an example of a regional institution. BOCES provides a wide variety of services in special education, staff development, and computer technology, and it also provides library media related services.

The input of the taxpayer also varies. In some states, the taxpayers vote directly on the passage of the school district budget. In other states, while there may be hearings, the taxpayer can directly affect the process only by voting for the person who will serve on the school board or the county commissioner's board. In states where people in these positions are appointed rather than elected, individual taxpayers have even less say over the approval of expenditures for educational purposes.

It is important to understand the political structure of school districts in your state. Although that process may be removed from the day-to-day functioning of the school, being informed about the process may guide the language that you use in a budget presentation. It will also help you understand the degree to which the individual taxpayer has control over the school budget, or more importantly, the perception of the taxpayer regarding that control.

Regardless of the structure; regardless of whether the school district budget is passed by the school board and then again by the commissioners or whether it is controlled by the legislators; regardless of whether or not the school board has direct financial authority over the budget, in general, school districts get money from the public by some form of taxation.

The process by which money gets from the pockets of the taxpayers into resources and services in the teacher's classroom is usually a decision at the state level. Some states use sales tax as a form of funding schools, others use real estate tax. In some states, all tax money goes to the state level, and then decisions are made regarding how much money a school district needs to educate its student, and the state sends that much money to the localities. In other states, the tax money comes directly into the school district coffers from the taxpaying public.

It is generally recognized that there are four functions in the fiscal operations of the school district: planning, implementation, evaluating, and reporting. Figure 3.1 illustrates this in more detail.

Figure 3.1: Budget Functions

The Budget Functions

Planning	The process that an organization goes through to produce the budget.
Implementing	Spending of the funds that are included in the budget.
Evaluating	Comparing the process that resulted in the budget with the processes of budgets past.
Reporting	Using statistics to summarize budget activities.

Planning refers to the process that results in the published budget. Each school district has an outlined budget process that details the deadlines, the policies, and the procedures that the district follows as it prepares the annual budget. This process must be available as public information. Although more and more districts have the budget procedure manual online, a hard copy is usually found in each school. Implementation refers to the acquisition procedures that guide the spending of the monies in the final approved budget. The implementation phase covers one fiscal year, which for school districts is usually July 1st to June 30th. Evaluation looks at the process that produced the budget in comparison to the effect that the budget had, and reporting is the process of producing fiscal reports and statistics on how the money was spent.

Of these functions, planning encompasses the greatest variation from district to district. Somehow, according to established district procedures, requests for funds are channeled through processes, approvals, signatures, and other means to culminate in a published document that is the school district budget. This process is carefully documented in a budget policy and procedures manual. It is important to scan through the school district as well as the state-level budget policy and procedures manual. The deadlines, procedures, lines of authority, and other information are extremely valuable to a library media specialist working on budget strategy.

It is important to realize that the proposed budget can only be affected during the planning process. Once passed and in the implementation phase, the budget cannot be changed without returning to the taxpayers for permission. This is usually based in state law and is strictly adhered to in most districts.

Although evaluation is mentioned as a fiscal function, most school districts may only give the budget process a cursory evaluation, if they do at all. The budget process may be an informational item on the school administrative team's agenda, but it is mostly used to report on progress or to announce the completion of the cycle. Very few districts conduct an in-depth evaluation of whether the process as implemented maximized the budgeting effort. Even fewer districts attempt to tie the budget process to student achievement or to other educational outputs.

The reporting function is an important but mostly automated function that produces statistics according to stated criteria for district, state, and national reports. However, with the current emphasis on accountability, the reporting function may be used in different ways in the future to assess the money spent with any corresponding increase in student test scores or to report on building projects or new programs.

As noted previously, the fiscal year is usually July 1st until June 30th. All monies contained in a budget for a particular year must be spent or at least encumbered (meaning that purchase orders have been written and the items are on order) by June 30th. Any unspent money is used to reduce the tax burden required by the next budget or is placed in special accounts that can be built up year after year, such as capital accounts to prepare for building new schools or repair existing ones.

It is not unusual for districts to create a deadline, a date by which funds must be encumbered; often, this is much earlier than the end of the fiscal year. Even though June 30th is the fiscal year ending date, the deadline for orders may be as early as mid-February. This gives plenty of time for the acquisitions processes to be completed, the to be materials received, and the bills to be paid.

Obviously, some materials necessary for the operation of the school district are ordered after the deadline, but use of the deadline avoids a last minute rush for the accounting office. If an order is cancelled at the last minute and is too close to the end of the fiscal year, the money may not have time to be encumbered for a different purpose.

The accounting and budgeting process usually does not vary from district to district and certainly does not vary much within the district from school to school. Somewhere in the district, probably in the principal's office, is a written procedure for how the budget is developed and expended. A school district budget uses codes for certain types of items. Library books may be code 506 or code 7284. Equipment repair is another code. Generally, codes are bundled into programs; an administrator in the district is given the responsibility to budget for all of the codes within that program. An example of a possible budget code structure is shown in Figure 3.2.

Figure 3.2: Budget Codes

Budget Code: 474 54 506 5493 93

	Library Program	Specific School	Type of Item	Item Number	Person To Whom Materials Will Be Delivered
Budget Code	474	54	506	5493	93

Chapter 3: Understanding Budget Terms and Processes

Administrators are usually given budget parameters, and the administrators then develop a budget accordingly. The finished budget may be thousands of pages, with lines such as the one presented in Figure 3.2. Very rarely is the budget reviewed line by line after it is developed because of the sheer amount of data and detail involved. A budget review is usually lumped by program, by school, or even by level in large districts. Once you have convinced someone to add money to your budget, chances are it will stay there. Think of it this way. If the total instructional materials budget in your district is $500,000, which may be a small figure for a medium-sized school district, how much difference will it make if you can convince someone to raise that figure to $505,000? That increase makes almost no difference to the individual taxpayer; nonetheless, it may make an incredible difference in your library program and to your students and staff.

There are two ways for money to be added to the budget. One way, commonly used for library books, is the "lump sum" approach. A lump sum is a pool of money designated for a particular type of expense. You may have been told that you have been allocated $5,000 for library books. You will simply submit purchase requisitions, usually with a variety of different vendors, until the money is spent. A "line item," on the other hand, is a specific material from a specific vendor. Equipment is sometimes purchased in this way. A line item contains the item name (three overhead projectors), the vendor (AV, Inc.), and the amount ($1,200). With lump sums, as long as money exists, the library media specialist can spend it, within the designated category of course. With line items, however, the decision is different. The school board did not agree that $1,200 could be spent on overhead projectors. Rather, the board agreed that three overhead projectors could be purchased. If the total bill comes to $900, most likely, the remaining money cannot be spent without permission and will go back in school district coffers to reduce the tax burden for the next school year.

Which is "safer," meaning which is more likely to remain in the budget in tough budget times, line items or lump sums? It depends. Line items are more easily reduced (cut your budget by 10%). On the other hand, a budget with a large number of line items will look a lot larger (more pages) as compared to a budget containing only lump sums.

School library media specialists must become familiar with the district procedures that guide budget development. The budget manual is not an exciting read and is usually fraught with budget jargon, deadlines, and descriptions of procedures and process. However, it would be a wise move to scan the document for any insight into how money moves in the district. Try to find out which administrators have budget control and which budget lines could possibly turn into funding streams for library media programs and services.

Effect of School Reform

Managerial strategies taught in business school inevitably make their way to the education arena, regardless of their successes or failures in the business world. An important resource for understanding the drive to manage a school on business terms is Calahan's *Education and the Cult of Efficiency* (1962). In this work, Calahan traces the change from schoolwork as the work of intellectuals to schoolwork as a function of business. This trend continues, and the waves of school reform reflect that continued trend (Verstegen, 1994). In business and industry during the 1980s and 1990s, theories such as "Total Quality Management" and "Zero Defects" focused on erasing the management layers that separated the worker from the decision-making process. Business theorists postulated that it was the worker who was best suited for making decisions to increase productivity. Management, especially upper-level management, could become out of touch with the manufacturing process and could make decisions that could hurt production, rather than help it. As with many business management theories, these reforms eventually were transferred to school administration. We will address two of these theories (site-based management and school-based management) most likely to affect the budget process in this chapter.

As you many recall from Chapter 2, site-based management gives decision-making power—power that traditionally belongs to the principal—to a team of teachers, parents, and other school personnel. Site-based management (SBM) in many schools has had a dramatic impact on the budget process. In some districts, individual budget codes have been collapsed into broad areas such as "instructional materials," or "supplies," meant for the entire school, rather than targeted for individual programs. Although in theory this may mean that the site-based management committee now has control over these large sums, it may also mean that budget authority is removed from the lowest level of administration, the principals and direct line supervisors, to a central office administrator. Still, the instructional supervisor or the principal will lobby for amounts to be included in the block category. It is important to identify how the lump sums coming into the school are budgeted and who has the authority to determine what those sums are.

It may seem as though site-based management may have accomplished just the opposite of its intention. If the intention was to place budget authority at the implementation level, then removing budget responsibility from the hands of the school library media specialist in charge of the school library media program defeats that purpose. Principals may have had more control over the budget streams that affect the school before site-based management was implemented. In some cases, that is true. Remember, however, the four functions of budgeting. In some schools, all the functions have been delegated to the SBM committee. However, in other districts, only the implementation function has been delegated, and the planning function has been removed to a higher level. Before approaching a site-based management team for budget reasons, it is important to understand the extent of its authority over the budget functions.

In theory, the four functions of budgeting (planning, implementing, evaluating, and reporting) are used to accomplish three main goals: control the school district funds, offer a fair distribution among the variety of school programs and student and staff needs, and maintain the efficiency and the effectiveness of results. Site-based management applied to the budget process may be concentrated on the planning function, in an attempt to make that function reflect more accurately the needs of the school (fairness). Total control is usually reserved for administrative authority.

When site-based management enters into the process, it is as an attempt to increase the achievement of the budget goals. In order to be truly effective, the site-based management committee should not only have an understanding of budgeting but also an understanding of school-wide programs and processes as well as the impact of the budget functions on those programs. There is great variety among schools regarding the authority of the SBM committee relative to the four budgeting, functions. Some committees are restricted to evaluation, investigating the impact of each budget cycle on school achievement. Some are greatly involved in planning, to the extent that all budget requests may have to go through the SBM committee. Very few committees are involved in the preparation of budget reports, although they may review them as part of the evaluative process. The degree to which the site-based management committee is involved in implementation varies as well.

Figure 3.3 illustrates some ways in which the school library media specialist can articulate budget needs to show an understanding of the four budget functions (planning, implementing, evaluating, reporting) and the four budget goals (fairness, efficiency, effectiveness, control). The figure pairs a budget goal with a budget function. However, in general, fairness, efficiency and effectiveness, and control impacts should be demonstrated for each function.

Figure 3.3: Relationship of the Site-Based Management Team and the School Library Media Budget Process

	Possible SBM Activities	SLMS Response	Impact
Planning	Prepare the school budget request	Make budget proposal to SBM committee	Fairness—the school library media budget will be substantially larger than other programs
Implementing	Allocate budgeted funds	Request funds tied directly to instructional programs	Results (efficiency)—the school library media dollar stretches to cover the entire school
Evaluating	Determine the effect of previous year's budget on school achievement	Share research on the impact of school library media programs on academic achievement	Results (effectiveness)—the school library media program can show effective results
Reporting	Review fiscal reports	Prepare fiscal reports matching budget allocations to state and national data	Control—the school library media program consistently expends funds in specific areas (books, periodicals, etc.)

As noted, if the SBM team performs the budget planning function, then the school library media specialist will be making the budget proposal to the SBM team. The school library media specialist will have to rationalize the size of the school library media budget in relationship to other program areas. Since the SBM team may be allocating any lump sums, it would be wise to emphasize that every dollar spent on the library media program benefits each teacher and each student in the school. It is efficient to expend money on the library media program since it covers the entire school. An effective library media program is crucial to the education of each student. The school library media specialist, as a trained manager, is trained in the acquisition of materials. These are just some of the ways that the library media program can be shown to be fair, efficient, effective, and under control. Brainstorm other ways to show why the school library media program emphasizes fairness, efficiency and effectiveness, and control mechanisms.

A budget-savvy school library media specialist will use the budget principles and goals to exploit the budget process to benefit the school library media programs. Words such as "fair," "equitable," and "effective" have both social and economic connotations. One book placed in a school library media center collection has the potential to be read by all students in the school. A book placed in a classroom collection, while it may be shared, is intended for the students in that class only. Using an analogy or a metaphor, such as "touches every child," the visual of one dollar stretching to cover the entire school instructional process, as well as other images can greatly enhance a budget presentation to the SBM committee.

Even in schools without strong site-based management committees or in those in which the SBM team does not have a substantial degree of budget involvement, the functions of the budget process may still have been decentralized to the school level. In some districts, funding for all personnel, instructional materials, supplies, equipment, and professional development funds could be under the control of the school administrative team. The building principal may then have control over the four fiscal functions.

With limited time, limited energy, and limited resources, it is essential that the effort spent by the school library media specialist in the preparation of the school library media budget request is directed at the correct audience. Do you know who has budget authority over the library program in your school and district? If there is a library supervisor in your district, quite possibly he or she budgets for all the libraries. But this is not necessarily so. There are many positions that might have authority over the library program. It could be the building principals, each with budget authority over all codes pertaining to that particular school. It could be the instructional supervisors, each with budget authority over the codes pertaining to that particular subject area. It could even be an assistant superintendent, making decisions for all programs. Sometimes the authority is divided, with the principal maintaining some codes and the instructional supervisor maintaining others. What budget functions does the site-based management team perform? Even if the SBM team only hears a report from the building principal on the budget process, this could be interpreted as sharing the budget function of evaluation. In some districts, a combination of all the possibilities mentioned could be in place. Here again, the school district policy and procedures manual will be extremely helpful.

For schools using site-based management to decide how funds are expended, generally a designated administrator may still have final authority on how much money will be requested in the budget process. Remember, however, although the administrator may have the authority to approve or deny budget requests, most likely he or she is not the one who sits at the computer screen tapping at the keys. It is more likely that there is a secretary or a support staff person who sits at the keyboard and types numbers into budget codes at budget development time. That person can have a huge influence on the decisions made by the budget administrator.

School-based management may have an interesting impact on equity decisions. From school to school, wide variations may occur in programs or positions depending on the decision-making authority of the budget administrator. There are important questions to ask. Could a school administrator or an SBM team decide not to have a school library media specialist, but instead have a technology consultant? Could money for library books be used to build classroom libraries? Who decides how much money will be typed into the budget request for school library media programs in your district? Who can you influence to type numbers into codes for your library program?

The school district budget procedure manual will answer many of the aforementioned questions. Obtain a copy of the manual from your office. Scan it frequently, and look carefully to understand the outline of the budget process as it pertains to the school library media program. Pay particular attention to administrative newsletters and to newspaper articles reporting on school board meetings. Talk to office clerical staff to be sure that you understand the budget procedures in your district. The more you understand the procedure, the greater your chances of presenting a successful budget.

Types of Budgets

There usually is some type of budget philosophy in a school district. Most of these philosophies, reduced to sound-bite phrases, come straight from the business world. A quip tossed around in the 1980s was that it took 10 years for a management process to transfer from the business world to the government sector, which was about the time that business was deciding that it didn't work and was moving on to something else. The types of budgets that follow have all been used in the business world at one time or another. Although many have come and gone, and some are used mainly in theory and not in practice, it is good to review the basic definitions here.

Zero-Based Budgets

Zero-based budgets begin each year with the premise that the year starts with a clean slate, with a zero. All programs have to be re-justified as if the program were being initiated for the first time. There are three main reasons for using zero-based budgeting. One, district administrators can review the successes of each program. Two, programs that are unsuccessful are more obvious. And three, even programs central to the educational mission of the district are forced to reexamine strategies and achievements. If some programs have fallen short of their claims for student achievement, or if district priorities have changed, money can be reallocated according to the new priorities.

Although there are benefits, zero-based budgets take a lot of time to develop and defend. In the school setting, if zero-based budgeting is used exclusively, much of this development time is spent defending programs that are basic to the education structure, such as the core curricular subject areas. Although in theory this forces program area administrators to take a critical look at the way instruction is delivered and at the reasons behind instructional choices, in reality, the same defense is usually copied from the previous year's budget defense with little changes.

PPBS: Planning, Programming, Budgeting System

Previous to the onset of school-based management, the most common type of budgeting was program-based budgeting. The most common budget was the one developed for the Department of Defense: the Planning, Programming, Budgeting System (PPBS). PPBS budgets are similar to zero-based budgets in that they are based on programs, rather than individual budget lines.

In program-based budgeting, the school district is supposed to set priorities and decide which programs will be funded. Program administrators make a statement of goals with evaluative criteria, and then each program under those priorities is cost out so that school district knows the exact dollar figures for each program. The theory is that if the school district needs to cut corners, the lowest priority may be cut, and so on.

In PPBS, the library program could be seen as separate and distinct from other programs and may be more likely to be reduced or eliminated than others. However, it may be possible to present the library program budget as support for all other budgets in the school. Some school library media specialists have taken this one step further by breaking down each acquisition request into subject areas. Figure 3.4 shows how it may be possible to turn a traditional program budget into one that is tied to other program areas. Note that the neotraditional program budget only gives a few examples. In reality, every program area, including all curricular areas as well as those such as the school lunch program, transportation, and administration, would be supported by the school library media budget.

Figure 3.4: Comparison of School Library Media PPBS Budget

Traditional Program Budgets		Neotraditional Program Budgets	
Library Books	$234,000	Science Program	$ 35,000
Audiovisual	123,000	Math Program	68,000
Equipment	206,000	Language Arts Program	98,000
Staff – LMS	302,000	Social Studies Program	123,000
Staff – Clerical	183,000	Professional Growth Program	15,000
Central Library Office	154,000		

In the "Traditional Program Budgets" column in Figure 3.4, it is easier to see how an administrative decision could be made to cut all library clerks in order to save the district $183,000. The decision could also be to cut the figure in half or by a certain percentage. Contrast that budget with the "Neotraditional Program Budgets" column. The library media program budget is broken down into subject areas and reflects the support of the library media program for each of these areas, including the work of library clerical staff, the central library office, and resources. It is more difficult to eliminate a library support staff position if it can be shown that 20% of staff time supports the reading initiative, 10% assists with special education students in the library, and so on.

This type of budget is far more work to prepare. It is very difficult to figure out just how much of each staff member's time is in support of each program area. In concept, this is similar to an attorney's "billable hours." However, faced with the decision to cut support for math versus science, administrators may well turn to another program to make the cuts. The neotraditional program budget also shows the school-wide effect of the library media program. If school library media supervisors had used this concept to show how the centralized school district library services supported each program in the school, we may have had more library supervisors left over from the Elementary and Secondary Education Act era. Note also that although this is time-consuming to develop the first year, the development in each ensuing year can be made with minor modifications.

Performance Budgets

Performance-based budgets are a direct result of the emphasis on accountability. It is an admitted weakness that traditional school budgets are not necessarily determined by evaluation of programs, but instead they are based on per-pupil formulas, a continuation of budget categories, and negotiated items, such as teacher salaries. Performance-based budgets in industry make each program accountable in terms of its effectiveness to the business goal of bottom-line profit. That is more difficult to do in the education arena.

Most would agree that the input-output method works well in business. In Florida, performance-based budgeting was mandated for state agencies, with some success. However, education is not as easily organized. Financial resources are not the only input in educational processes, and accountability is difficult to measure. Providing incentives for efficient use of resources, and disincentives for inefficient use, could work fairly well. However, performance-based budgeting works best when programs are targeted with clear, measurable goals, such as dropout prevention, increasing the number of students attending college, and other programs outside of the instructional day.

One impact of using performance-based budgeting may be more flexibility in allocation of funds, with more lump sums replacing a long list of line items. This gives the organization flexibility to spend money in order to maximize outcomes for the organization.

There is a benefit to performance-based budgeting as well as a danger. Educational outcomes are affected by an incredibly wide range of variables. Holding the school library program accountable for the school achievement goals is questionable. However, it may be possible to target new programs that can be placed in the performance-based budgeting systems. Although these programs would benefit the entire school library program, they can also be school-wide initiatives that otherwise may not be funded. Figure 3.5 shows some examples of the possibilities.

Figure 3.5: Performance-Based School Library Media Programs

Possible Performance-Based Programs for School Libraries

Goal	Impact	Accountability
Increase reading	Purchase books and other reading materials, have special programs or speakers, renovate facility to create reading areas.	Test scores, student surveys, circulation statistics
Information skills	Staff development on collaboration, increased staff, increased technology.	Test scores, changes in student assignments
Retention of new teachers	Create teacher mentor section in the library, increase professional books, assist with staff development.	Increase in retention of new teachers

With Figure 3.5, the individual components of the library media program could be broken into sub-programs, each with a clear goal. If the goal was not achieved, it could be argued that the program was not funded at a high enough level. If the goal was achieved, it could be argued that the increase in test scores was directly related to the increase in the allocation for library books, as an example. With the large number of variables that could have affected test scores, tying any increase to the library media program without the strictest of research guidelines would be almost impossible to prove. However, it would also be almost impossible to disprove.

Using performance budgets to fund school districts is unwieldy, since the processes that are necessary to educate students are numerous and overlapping. However, for special projects such as those in Figure 3.5, performance-based budgeting has definite appeal.

Percentage Increase

Preparing a budget by an across-the-board percentage increase would not be advocated by any finance textbook. Yet, this is the reality for the budget processes in many school districts. A school district may profess to use a particular budget preparation method but will still give percentage guidelines to the budget administrators. The bottom line for taxpayers is simple. How much the budget has increased over the previous year's figure, and how much their taxes will increase? This is most easily explained with percentage increases.

Regardless of the budget process used, a school library media specialist should be aware of the preferred budget preparation method. Reading school board minutes, newspaper accounts of school board meetings or interviews with the superintendent, or simply listening carefully at faculty meetings when school budgets are discussed will give clues as to the district's philosophy of budgeting. Budget preparation tends to be conservative, and it may wise to align the library media budget with the stated budget process of the school district and to make sure it is prepared and presented in the same way. However, an innovative approach might also work, depending on the audience to whom the budget will be presented. Knowing the audience is crucial.

The Budget Timeline

Regardless of the budgeting method used, the timeline is roughly the same in each district. Almost as soon as the fiscal year begins, the following year's budget cycle begins. Well before the end of the calendar year, usually in November or early December, budget requests will need to be submitted. The first rough draft of the new budget will be available in January or February, and the school board will begin budget work sessions during that time as well. The budget will be passed by the school board sometime in early spring and will be presented for passage in April or May to either the governing body of the municipality, or in some states, to the voters.

Once the budget is passed, orders can begin to be prepared, and requests for anything needed before the first day of school are prepared and submitted. At the turn of the fiscal year, the cycle begins again. This means that library media program requests will need to be identified very early in the cycle, almost a year or more in advance.

This is why budget cycles need to be continuous. Money is being requested, expended, and lobbied for at the same time. It is truly not one cycle, but rather a chain of interlocking cycles. The reasons behind these cycles lie not in the nuts and bolts of the budget but in the larger field of the macroeconomic view of school district finance.

The Big Picture

The basic premise of any economic system is supply and demand. When the system works well, both the buyer and the seller are better off after the transaction than before. The seller receives financial gain for a product, and the buyer receives a product that is needed or wanted. This is the perfect market principle in action. Students in basic economic theory classes compose graphs to show the supply-demand curve as well as impacts on the market, such as competition.

Business members in the community and on the school board, and some legislators contemplating new education policy, frequently compare education to the business sector. Mutters of complaints from the taxpayers to balance the school district budget are based on the premise that the taxpayers are buying a product (education) that the school district is selling (by receiving taxes).

There are some basic principles to the perfect market. Some of these are explained in more detail.

- **Large Numbers of Buyers and Sellers**—When there are large numbers of buyers and sellers, competition results. This forces sellers to keep prices competitive, and it forces buyers to choose between sellers. This leads to the next market principle.
- **Homogeneous Product**—In a perfect market, it is assumed that all products of the same type are equal. Buying from one seller is equal to buying from another seller. Therefore, sellers are forced to compete for the buyer's dollars by either producing a superior product, lowering the price, or both.
- **Perfect Information**—Perfect information means that sellers know everything there is to know about buyers and their need for the product and that buyers know everything there is to know about sellers and the making of the product.

One commonly heard use of market principles in education policy is in the development of voucher systems and charter schools. Part of the reason education is assumed to be in trouble is that there is not enough competition for the public education dollar. Increasing the number of sellers of education, it is assumed, will force public schools to increase the quality of their product.

The usual defense against this is to decry the use of market theory by stating that children are not widgets to be manufactured on an assembly line and that the market system cannot be applied. However, the quasi-economists and business people on the school board and among the taxpayers will see that as a weak claim because there is no such thing as a perfect market. There are never enough buyers and sellers, products are never homogeneous, and there is no such thing as perfect information. Something is always not known, and therefore, the claim that children are special and must be educated as such is not a strong argument, even though it may be philosophically sound.

A better defense is to explain each principle using the education system. There are a large number of buyers, but the American education system is not one seller. The comprehensive public school offers many options to many students. If we knew what our one educational "product" was, perhaps we would have a better chance of explaining why education is not homogeneous. Our product could be the college acceptance rate, except that some students choose a different path. It could be the need to prepare students for trade jobs, except that is not the best choice for all students. The best explanation, perhaps, is that our product cannot be considered homogeneous because our raw materials—our students—are not homogeneous. We will always be struggling for more information, better educational evaluation methods, and better instruction to help each student succeed in terms of how success can be measured.

School libraries are also vulnerable to attacks based on the market theory. From time to time, the reason for a community having both a public library and a school library is discussed. This is seen as a duplication of effort and a waste of taxpayers' money. Instead of seeing the school and public libraries as good concepts, i.e., increasing the available sellers of library materials to the consuming public, some believe that the public is forced to buy a homogeneous product from two different sellers.

Some adults also believe that the way they used libraries as children is still the way libraries operate now. Others believe that the operation they see when they use a library—the checking out and returning of library materials—is the only library operation of significance. There are books in both places, and the check-in and check-out operations happen at both places. There are children using both types of libraries. Therefore, the duplication seems obvious.

Two different principles of the market theory are applied here. First, it is believed that there is a homogeneous product, and second, it is believe that there is perfect information, in other words, the taxpayer and the school decision makers know everything there is to know about the purpose and the operation of libraries.

We can rant and whine about not being understood, and we can defend the rationale for the school and public libraries in emotional terms. However, the only truly successful way to discuss an economic argument is to return to market theory and to develop an argument based on economic terms.

There are reasons why school library media centers and public libraries do not share a homogeneous product. The answer lies in the curriculum of the school library media center and the role of the school library media specialist as a teacher of information literacy skills. It is obvious that there is no perfect information at work here, which offers the opportunity to discuss the different missions, operations, and purposes of the school library media center and the public library. Not only are the school and public library created differently with different missions, the "buyers" of the services are different as well. School library media centers serve the students and the teachers in the school, both those who willingly walk into our doors and those we have to go out and find. Our mission, and therefore our accountability, extends to every student in the school. Public libraries, while there are many services and programs that can be shared, have a different mission, and consequently, have both a different product and a different customer (buyer) base.

When market theory is used to diminish the ability of the school library media program to offer programs and services, the only possible defense is to use the principles of market theory to combat these reasons. The same arguments can be used to explain, for example, why classroom libraries are of great benefit to the school but cannot supplant budget allocations to the school library media center.

When Government Plays a Market Role

Most economists believe that, in general, government should stay out of market interactions. The role of government in the free market is basically to make as few rules as possible and then to make sure everyone is playing by those rules. The less intervention from government, the more the supply and demand curves can operate freely within the market principles.

Sometimes, however, a failure of the market forces government intervention. This happens for a number of reasons. First, the goods or services may be too socially important to be left to market forces. Education and libraries certainly qualify under these guidelines. Another reason: the market forces create unfairness for one or more groups of buyers or sellers. Again, education certainly qualifies. The market forces may operate quite well in some socioeconomic areas but will fail miserably in others.

Government can force communities to support quality education for all children in two ways (Bosworth, 2001). The first is by funding. The federal government funds many of the special education programs, provides nutritious meals for children whose families cannot afford to provide them, and at one time in our history, provided funds to build school library collections.

Governments also force action by regulation. Many school library media specialists argue for government mandates for a professional school library media specialist in every school. Although this could happen without funding, it is unlikely without substantive arguments that there is inequity in the educational system when some schools have a professional library media specialist and some do not. Although there is validity to this argument, it is rarely heard.

As federal funding again becomes a reality, it is important to look at Elementary and Secondary Education Act funding in terms of government intervention. School library materials are socially important goods that are distributed unfairly. Some schools, because of wealth or a high tax base, contribute more to school library resources than other schools. The taxpayers suffer indirectly from this neglect as schools produce graduates who may not be good readers or graduates that were exposed to a general lack of educational quality. However, the children suffer directly, which is a strong case for government intervention.

Production Function Economics

Production function, in economics, refers to the relationship between inputs and outputs. Think of any manufacturing process. Raw materials (inputs) go through some sort of manufacturing process and are turned into products (outputs). The production function equation describes the money that can be made from the process of turning inputs into outputs. In general, this equation is the measure of the amount of output that can be produced by one unit of labor (Ladd & Hansen, 1999, p.135). By figuring out ways to reduce the price of the inputs and by finding different and less expensive ways to run the production process, more profit can be made from the outputs.

This is easy to illustrate with any manufacturing assembly. Think of the automobile industry. The individual parts of the car are either manufactured in-house or are purchased at the cheapest price. Then the car is assembled through a production process. Inputs (car parts) go through an assembly line (process) and are turned into for-sale cars (outputs). Automobile manufacturers constantly figure out ways to reduce the costs of their inputs, either by substituting different materials (vinyl instead of leather) or by buying the materials from less expensive sources. They search for ways to reduce the costs of the production process, sometimes by moving the entire process to another state or country to find lower labor costs. Sometimes this reduces the price of the outputs to the customer, and sometimes the profits stay with the manufacturer.

Does education have a production function? Most researchers in this area would hesitate but would eventually say, "Yes." Despite the frequently heard claims that a school should be run like a business, and that business leaders, not education leaders, should run school districts, there are obvious difficulties with using the manufacturing production function model.

- **Inputs**—What are the educational inputs? Would it be students, or would it be student characteristics and demographics, such as family educational background, socioeconomic level, or even marital status of the parents? We of course need to include money as an input. But what about non-monetary items, such as curricula, teacher skills and experience, student motivation, or even administrative factors?
- **Process**—Are curricula and teacher skills inputs or processes? The educational production function process should probably be the entire teaching and learning process, but that includes some factors that are clearly inputs and some that are clearly outputs.
- **Outputs**—Are outputs test scores, graduation rates, or some other level of education behavior? What about previous test scores that are sometimes used in placement for future educational services? Do those become part of the inputs, part of the process, or are they still outputs? How about qualitative outputs, such as lifelong learners or educated citizens? How can those be evaluated in quantitative terms? In some ways, the inputs themselves are also outputs. Reading a book, for instance, is valued for the effect of reading on academic achievement. However, reading is also valued for the experience of reading as well as for the measurements of reading skill and comprehension.

Interest in the education production function was spurred by the release in 1966 of an Office of Education study on equity of educational opportunity (Coleman, 1966). Nicknamed "The Coleman Report," this massive study collected data from over 500,000 students and nearly 100,000 schools and teachers. The study found that there was little if any connection between educational spending and educational achievement. Following the release of this report, literally hundreds of researchers intensively studied elements of the connection between educational inputs and educational outputs.

The best known researcher in educational production function research is most likely Eric Hanushek. In 1989, Hanushek's article on the educational production function reviewed previous research on production function economics applied to education. Hanushek found that in almost all of the studies, there were very few factors that truly affected student achievement, and very few of these had to do with monetary inputs. He concluded that there was little or no evidence that there was a relationship between the amount of money spent on education and student achievement.

Other researchers have tried to show the effect of non-monetary inputs, such as demographics, or have identified a single input, such as the effect of a single program. However, this research must follow strict guidelines. It is very difficult to account for all of the factors that could affect the teaching and learning processes in the school.

With all the difficulties in articulating the education production function, why it is still being used? There are probably two main reasons. First, if the education production function does not apply, that means that there may be no way to justify any educational interaction that requires an increase in funding, because the only way to prove that a program works is to use a variation of production function economics. The second reason is for the efficient operation of the school district. Viewing the educational process as a production function assumes educational processes have a direct impact on student achievement. Regardless of whether or not the effect can be proven, the discussion of the education production function process is invaluable to program improvement.

The School Library Media Production Function

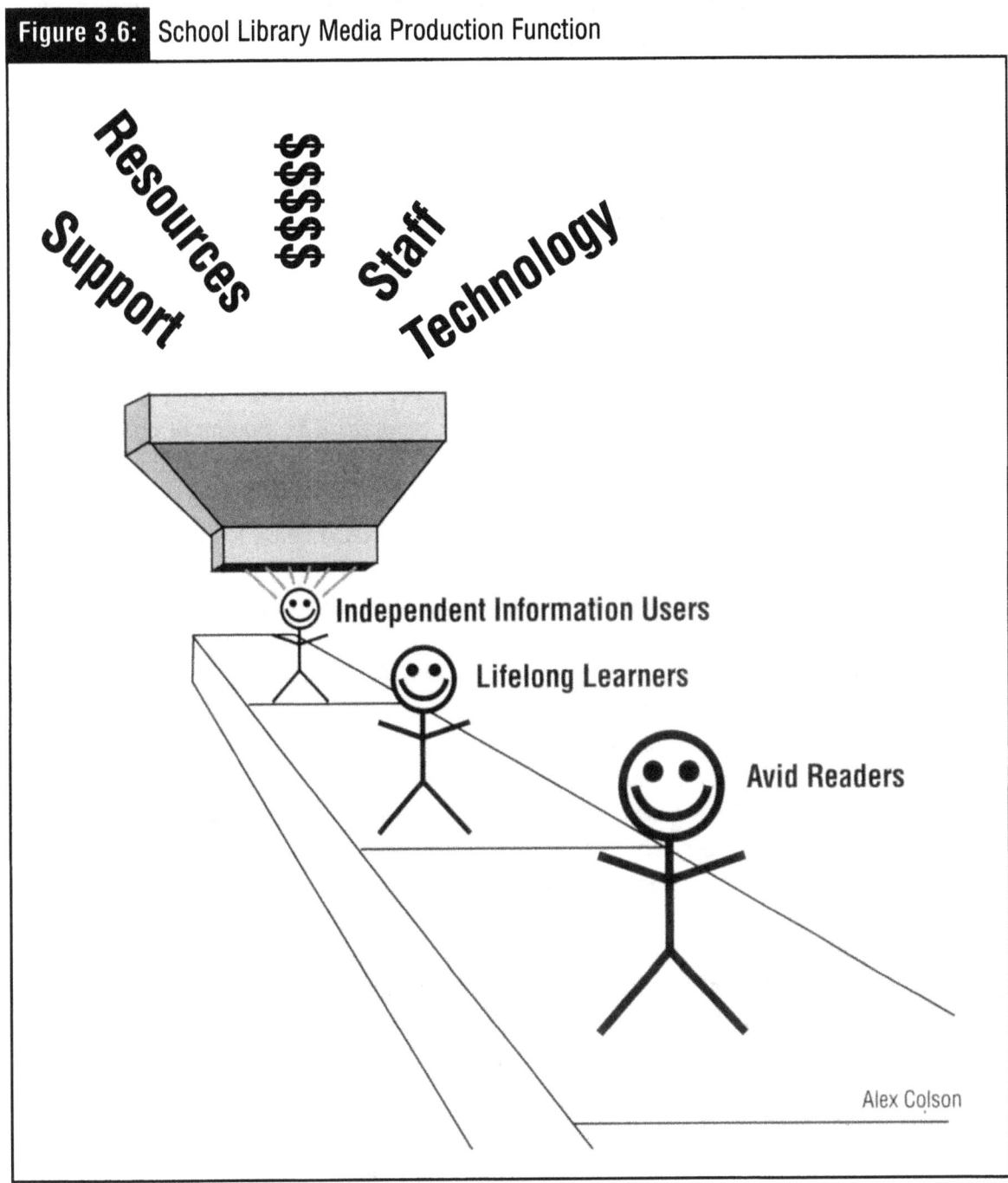

Figure 3.6: School Library Media Production Function

Alex Colson

In Figure 3.6, the identified inputs are support from administrators and classroom teachers, money, library media staff, resources, and technology. These, along with inputs based on the student population and the classroom teacher experiences and skills, go through the school library media program process. Our identified outputs, then, are independent information users, lifelong learners, and avid readers.

In order to justify the educational expense of the school library media center, we know that we have to prove that we are central to the educational process. That means we have to be able to discuss the school library media production function and have to be able to articulate the relationship between inputs, school library media processes, and instructional outputs. Think about the details that follow.

- **Inputs**—In the school library media center, inputs can be divided into three categories. Some are direct monetary benefits, such as the budget items that are directly translated into resources including expenditures for library books, technology resources, and other library resource expenditure. The second is staff expenditures, the school library media specialists and support staff. The third input is based on program. Administrator support, staff interaction, and intangibles, such as a student's motivation and love of reading or information literacy experience, are included as well. Student demographic factors, such as whether or not they have a computer at home, may also be an input.
- **Process**—The program elements of the school library media center define the process in the school library media center program. The amount of collaboration in the information skills process, the degree and effort put into reading encouragement, and the advocacy program create a shared commitment to vision and are all part of the process. *Information Power* (AASL/AECT, 1998) is the articulation of the school library media process for our profession.
- **Outputs**—The outputs of the school library program are difficult to define. The impact on student achievement in all areas, including information literacy skills assessment, has been used in recent research. The constantly-used phrase "love of reading" should be assessed in this area as should the term "lifelong learner."

There is greater potential for the school library media production function to justify and explain the impact of the school library media center programs on student achievement. Previous research, such as the studies by Keith Curry Lance <www.lrs.org> and the very early research discussed in Chapter 2, has shown the impact of programs on student achievement. Much more research has to be conducted in this area. What is needed most is research focusing on specific elements of programs. Hanushek's research is powerful because he was able to use a variety of studies from different researchers to draw conclusions regarding education in general. We need the studies on a variety of areas for the foundation of our own school library media production function equation.

Funding Adequacy

This discussion leads inevitably to the concept of funding adequacy. Educators are just beginning to grasp the concept of funding adequacy. How much money does it take to educate a child? The factors, which may be very easy to standardize for industry, are almost impossible to control in education. How much money could it possibly take to educate each child is determined by another look at the education production function?

In industry, when a raw material is not up to standard, usually a process will have to be instituted to either fix the materials or to devise a change in the production that will fix the impact of the substandard materials. This is commonly referred to as a filter. Filters add cost to the production function equation. If a raw material is defective in a manufacturing process, additional materials may have to be used to correct the defect. It is much less expensive to buy quality raw materials in the first place than to implant a filter to fix substandard ones. This is a very logical conclusion for business and industry.

However, in education, the public school systems cannot control inputs. We have no control over whether or not a child's parents were poorly educated, went to college, are strong readers, or are supportive of the education process. We have to use the state-mandated curriculum, and although a school district can hire teachers, to some extent, the levels of experience and skills are beyond the individual principal's control. The innate aptitude and motivation of the child are certainly beyond the school's control.

Because of the variety of inputs into the education production function, schools can and do implement filters for the instructional process. Parent education programs to improve parent support, programs such as "Head Start," and remedial education programs are all filters that add cost to the process but also increase the value of educational outputs.

Because of the need for such a variety of filters, and because the education process has to be designed for the needs of each unique child, deciding how much money is needed is almost impossible. Even using previous research to formulate best guesses and other techniques makes this concept difficult.

Can we develop this concept of funding adequacy for the school library media center program? There are some recommended funding levels, but very few of these are based on research on funding adequacy. What constitutes a "good" collection? What number of materials, within what copyright date range, and in what formats, should a school library media center hold? What is the proper amount of technology? How much should be spent on reading encouragement programs? Until we have the answer to these questions, or at least have much more research into the area of collection development, it is difficult to delve into collection adequacy at the national level.

It may be easier at the building level. You can identify the inputs into the library media program. You can articulate the instructional process, can build a list of the filters that affect the school library media program in your school, and can relate these to the outputs of student achievement. In the next section, as you begin to develop the budget plan, the concept of funding adequacy will return as you identify the specific target budget figures.

Funding Equity

Unfortunately, the level of funding equity is extremely low in education. The level is lower still for programs, such as school library media, which have very limited mandated levels of inputs. There is extreme difference in the level of funding provided by different states, different school districts, and even for different schools within the same school district. Funding equity is divided into two areas: equity of educational opportunities and equity of educational outcomes.

Equity of educational opportunity is, on the surface, rather easy to achieve. For school library media programs, allocating equal dollars to all schools and buying the same number and type of resources can achieve this. In theory, this would ensure that each school library is funded to the same level as others, providing all students with the same opportunities to use resources. However, this would be true, in reality, if all schools were the same size. Per-pupil allotments benefit large schools but are insufficient for small schools. If a school district allotted $25 per pupil for library resources, a 2,000-student school would be allocated $50,000. A 1,000-student school would receive $25,000. Does a 2,000-student school need twice as many resources as a 1,000-student school? Suppose this same district had a very small school, perhaps 250 students. That would reduce this school's allocated amount to $6,250. Although having more students means that the collection needs to be larger, there is a certain level of core collection materials that would be the same regardless of size. Per-pupil allotment, although on the surface a way to achieve funding equity, quickly fails the equity test.

Difficulties arise when attempting to fund for equity in educational outcomes. If we believe that all students should love to read, what are the differing needs for different schools in different communities? A school in which most students are book owners, library card users, and strong readers may be in maintenance mode for student reading needs. However, schools in communities where students do not have access to books outside of school may require many more resources to compensate for the lack of resources available in the home.

Summary

School districts have both a finance policy and a fiscal policy. Finance policy is how the school district handles the budgeting and the accounting for the education of students. Included in the finance policy are rules and policies governing the budgeting process, procedures for acquisition of materials, and general past practices of when and how budget increases occur. Finance policy refers to how a school district handles its money.

In contrast, a school district's fiscal policy refers not to policies and procedures but to the philosophy behind the financing of educational programs. Finance policy is usually fairly easily obtained, since it is written in board policy manuals and budget procedure books. Fiscal policy, on the other hand, is usually never articulated but is the pattern over time by which educational program decisions are made.

School library media specialists need to be familiar with the district's finance and fiscal policies. Taxpayers need to be confident that the money from their pockets, the money that is being spent on materials, resources, staff, and services, is in competent hands. We need to walk, to talk, and to act as competent business-professionals.

Read the budget policy and procedures manual for the district. You may be told that you are the only person to ever ask for it, and some parts might be boring, but skim through it anyway. It will help you to understand the restrictions, and also the loopholes, surrounding the district's approach to the budgeting process.

Make your own school library media production function graphic. Keep adding filters, inputs, and outputs. Try to articulate the school library media program processes.

Figure out the cost efficiency of resources. Cost efficiency is the price of the resource divided by the number of uses. What is the cost efficiency of a library search station? Of a popular paperback or magazine? Of a research database? Cost efficiency is a way to talk about thousands of dollars in terms of pennies per student.

What Would Savvy School Library Media Specialists Do?

Savvy school library media specialists (SSLMS) know that money can always be transferred. Around the middle of May, it will be obvious what money will not be expended for that school year. A friendly chat with the principal may produce hundreds or even thousands of dollars available for use by the school library program. SSLMS always have a must-have project to catch the principal's interest. Even savvier school library media specialists can figure out which programs may have that money. A school district forced to cancel school because of weather may decide to use staff development days as snow make-up days. What a great time to pitch an idea for using staff development funds to revamp and expand the professional collection. What areas could your school possibly have budgeted funds that it did not use? How could you make use of that money?

Savvy school library media specialists know the budget timeline. They know when budget requests are being considered, and they know when an e-mail or quick visit to the principal's office may get another zero on the end of a budget line. They also know the deadline when all offices are scrambling to get their purchase requisitions in. The SSLMS can prepare an order and slip it in someone's box. Most budget administrators do not like leaving allocated budget funds unspent. If the money is not being spent on something else and the deadline approaches, it just might wind up in your lap.

Savvy library media specialists know and use economic terms when discussing budget requests. They understand market principles and use the school library media production function to explain the relationship between school library media allocations and academic achievement.

Savvy school library media specialists understand that school districts must follow the law. Therefore, when the principal says that lost book money must be turned into the central office, savvy school library media specialists comply uncomplainingly. However, savvy school library media specialists know that what goes into the central office one year can come back to them the next year. Therefore, SSLMS keep track of that amount and budget for it in a separate budget category.

Part 2

Planning

Figure 3.7: The Budget Cycle

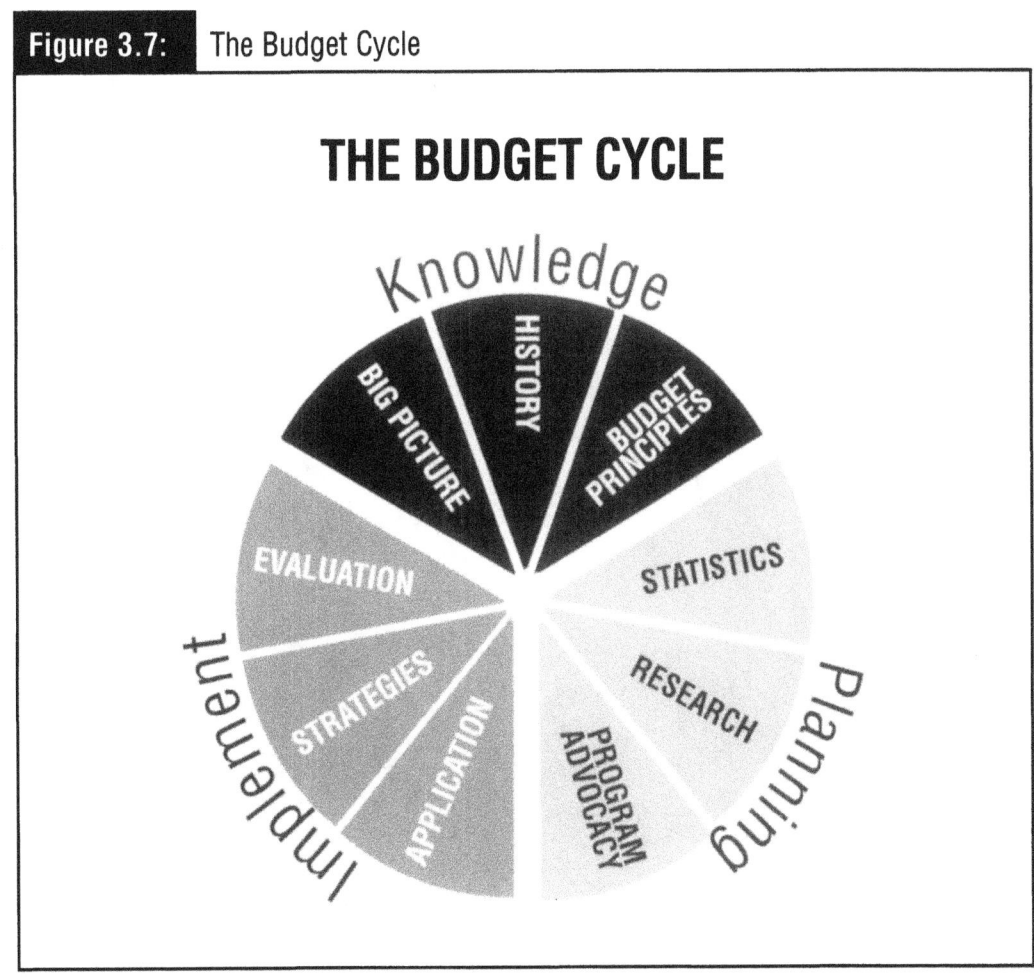

Up to this point, we have concentrated on background knowledge needed for the school library media administrative processes. We have focused on understanding big picture functions of the school district. We have looked at the history of the development and funding of school library media programs. We have also reviewed basic budget terms and processes.

In this part, we will apply that knowledge to the planning phase of budget development. As we begin to start forming the budget picture, it is crucial to develop a critical core of strong advocates for the program. Through action research and application of known statistics, we will begin to fill in the numbers for the budget plan. By the end of this section, you will have a well-developed and thoroughly planned budget.

Chapter 4

The Importance of Advocacy

Budgeting equals advocacy. The rewards that come from implementing a strong advocacy program can be measured in many ways, but the most direct way to measure the perceived value of the library media program is to measure the amount of funds budgeted in support of it. It is difficult to perceive of a process that will have a more direct impact on library media funding than spreading awareness of the place that the library media program has in the instructional life of the school. A strong, stable budget is one measure of the value that is placed on the library media program.

If advocacy can be defined as developing a strategy to get what you want, then we could easily define budgeting as developing a strategy to figure out what you want and how to get it. Every positive gain in an advocacy program advances the chance that your budget will be both approved and improved. Every time you have a successful special event, such as a parent reading night or a book fair, every time you update the teacher Web site, every time you do a monthly report for administrators, you are increasing the probability that your budget requests will get a favorable response.

Money goes to what your school and school district value. Specific programs that are priorities in the district may not be listed as such in the district mission statement or in a list of priorities. In fact, the goals that the district puts forth in written memos, in vision statements, and in priorities may be very different from what they actually fund.

Try this simple exercise to find out what is valued in your district. What new things have come into your district in the past several years? Complete Figure 4.1 for some insight.

Figure 4.1: What Does Your School District Value?

What Does Your School District Value?

How wealthy is your district?

☐ We have no money – never had, never will.

☐ We talk poor, but we usually get some things.

☐ We are considered a wealthy district, and most instructional items are ordered without question.

☐ We have lots of perks here. Money is no object.

Now make a list of the "stuff," such as new innovations, programs, equipment, renovations, that came in the district in the last several years.

Program School or Curriculum Area	New Stuff	What was the Stated Reason for Purchase

You may find that you have to continue on several sheets of paper to list new initiatives, renovations, or greatly increased levels of support for some programs. You may also find that regardless of the perception that faculty and staff may have of the district as being poor and barely able to afford the basics, quite a few new initiatives are coming into the district. How did that happen? And what are other people doing to get the support that you also deserve?

The center column in Figure 4.1 is relatively unimportant compared with the other two columns. What was purchased and how much was spent is not nearly as important as the information in the first and third columns. Which programs seemed to benefit the most? Why did the district decide to spend this money? Are there similarities in the stated reasons that are given to the taxpaying public? Are there specific programs that seemed to be funded more than others? Popular opinion seems to always paint the stereotypical picture that athletics are always being funded while libraries are never funded. However, thinking deeply about new buildings, renovations, new equipment, upgrades, new programs of study, new faculty members, and other curricular-related resources may provide more insight into the district funding priorities.

Now try to find some similarities among one of the columns. Is there a particular program area that seemed to be funded more than others? If there are truly no similarities, then focus on process. Is there a particular administrator or school board member whose support seems to count more than others? Maybe none of the aforementioned reasons apply. Perhaps it is as simple as the programs listed had a need, lobbied for the need to be recognized, presented their requests, and were funded. Whatever the reason, before launching time and energy into an advocacy program, it helps to understand where success has happened in the past. Then links to those people and programs that have been successfully funded can be created, and proven budget funding paths can be followed.

Try to avoid emotional or stereotypically whiny answers to the questions you are asking above. "They hate me," is probably not the reason you have not been funded. In a large district, a lack of funding may be the result simply of ignorance about the library program, not an active dislike. The reverse is also true. The school board may not fund a program because they like it. They may simply believe that the answer to a good school lies in a particular program. Or they may not realize the importance of a modern school library media program in academic achievement.

Changing their perceptions will change the pathways to support. Reflect on the backgrounds and life experiences of individual school board members and listen to their comments at school board meetings. What kinds of school experiences did they have in the past? What types of library experiences are they currently having? Do they seem to be making decisions based on their own school experiences or the school experiences of their children? Or are they making the decisions based on data and reports? Do some always accept and abide by the decisions of the superintendent? Do some always oppose the decision of the superintendent? What social issues seem to drive individual members?

Advocacy does not change the goals, the mission, or the vision of a program. Rather, advocacy is a strategy to achieve those goals and to make that vision a reality. It will be far more difficult to switch the mindset of the school district administration to funding libraries as a new concept than it will be to publicize how the library program fits into those issues and values already being funded.

An old wives' tale is of the milkmaid, who at the end of life, was asked why she never married. Her answer was, "No one ever asked me." Too often we are milkmaids, waiting to be asked. We have the initiatives that need to be funded in the district to achieve the district's vision. Sometimes, it is just as easy as asking the right people, in the right way, at the right time. Advocacy provides a strategy to do that.

What is Advocacy?

Advocacy has been a major issue in the American Library Association (ALA) and the American Association for School Librarians (AASL) for the last several years. "Library Advocacy Now" and the "@ Your Library" campaign are two of the more recent initiatives <www.ala.org>. These two major national initiatives have made tremendous strides in increasing awareness of the importance of libraries of all types.

While it is true that sometimes advocacy is measured by the amount of support the library receives, it is important to note that directly asking for funding is not a major or an overt part of these campaigns. Advocacy goes beyond financial support, and advocates do more than just support programs. They believe in the programs at a direct and passionate level. In other words, advocates care. Thousands of advocates are not needed to create change. A small core of five to 10 committed advocates for school library media programs will work wonders in the largest of school districts.

Advocacy is sometimes misnamed as either marketing or public relations (PR). It is neither, but advocacy does have elements of both of these strategies. Advocacy is more than public relations. The old public relations programs tended to center on a single issue. Creating sound bites designated to carry a single message was the focus of a PR campaign. In some ways, PR is also temporary, limited to the length of the issue. There may be a time limit to a campaign or a goal to sway public opinion on a certain issue. Advocacy creates believers in the program that underlies these time-sensitive issues. Advocacy is a long term, an across-the-board, multi-layered approach.

Advocacy is more than just marketing. Marketing is selling. It is transactional in nature, the exchange of a product (the library program) for support (increased budget). Weingand (1987) goes further to give a new definition of marketing. Rather than the old definition, which was close to the stereotype of advertising (getting people to want what they did not need), today's marketing works more to establish products that are based on individual needs. Marketing the library program focuses not on what the library has to offer, but rather it focuses on individuals and their perceived needs, which can be satisfied through libraries.

Modern advertising shows the power of the "I want" phenomenon. Through advertisement, it's easy to crave products and services that we had never heard of before and were doing fine without. A look at the unused gadgets and products on the top shelves of our kitchens is proof of the power of advertising. If we could create within individual taxpayers a "want" for school libraries, we would have a powerful force that would make the school library media program the top priority of the school community and the school board.

Advocacy goes even further than marketing, however. Advocacy is transformational. It changes the library program by creating deeper levels of involvement in the life of the school. Advocacy also changes the library supporters from just having a vote to having a voice in the library program. This makes the program go from belonging only to the school library media specialist to belonging to the school community.

Ownership must also transfer from the school library media specialist to the library community. The role of the school library media specialist changes from owner to that of facilitator and manager, implementing the school library media program dictated by the needs of the users. This will be very difficult for some school library media specialists, who through their actions show that they believe the role of the school library media program in the school is preservation, not education. Ask yourself which is more important, that students learn to treat materials carefully and return them on time or that they learn to use them?

Advocacy is based on the mission and beliefs of the school library media program. Figure 4.2 should look familiar. It is based on the figure that you completed in Chapter 1, with an additional column added. Take out Figure 1.2 from Chapter 1 and think about those people in the school and district who share your beliefs. What other faculty, administrators, staff, or people in the taxpaying community, including members of the parent teacher association, other parents, or school board members share those beliefs?

Figure 4.2: Advocating the Vision

Advocacy Exercise Questions from Figure 1.2	Additional Questions Table 4.2
1. Write down some words and phrases that "deep down" represent what you feel about the interaction of students and libraries. _____	Who feels the same way? _____
2. When you go home thinking, "this was a good day," what happened to make you feel that? _____	Who feels the same way? _____
3. Read the first chapter of *Information Power*. Write the mission of the library media program here. _____	Who will support this mission? _____
4. Your school district has a mission statement. Write it here. _____	Who already supports this mission? _____
5. Your school most likely has a mission statement as well. Write it here. _____	Who already supports this mission? _____
6. Write your school library mission statement. _____	Whose names have you written most often? Circle those who have a position of power or hold positions of authority in the school. _____

Advocacy is a planned, coordinated, and continuous effort to advance the library program; it is shared with a developed community of supporters. If a library program achieves progress in advocacy, think of how much simpler that shared and jointly-developed library budget is to present.

But how hard will it be to create strong advocates, and won't those activities take time away from the budgeting process? It is true that advocacy takes time. However, the time is not spent apart from the budgeting process. Although some of the benefits of advocacy are indirect and long-term, most school library media specialists report immediate effects as well.

Look at the sentence at the beginning of the previous paragraph again in conjunction with Figure 4.3. Figure 4.3 is a thinking worksheet, designed to start the thinking process about the advocacy program that is needed. Can you begin a budgeting program without a strong advocacy program? Certainly the act of preparing a budget request and submitting it to the proper office may produce some results, especially if that has never been done before. A new school library media specialist may find that the "honeymoon effect" of being new to the position could have budgetary benefits. However, the power of advocacy is long-term. Budgeting advocacy combined with a strong advocacy effort will produce far greater results, and those results will be more long-lasting.

Figure 4.3: Advocacy Overview

Advocacy is a

Planned	Planned by whom? Most advocacy strategists would say it should be planned by the representatives of the groups that would be affected. This means certainly other teachers, parents, maybe students. It should also include representatives of groups that we are trying to include as powerful partners. What are the groups in the community that are seen as powerful? It may be senior citizens or other community organizations. A program of advocacy planned by a partnership council will be much more effective than an advocacy program developed by a single person.
Coordinated	Who will do the work of coordinating this effort. Most likely, the school library media specialist has to be involved. It would be great if someone else can be the catalyst for making sure the advocacy wheel keeps turning, but most likely, your energy will need to be the spark.
Continuous	Continuous means never-ending. It could always mean ever-changing as well. Much will be achieved, but each success will reveal new areas, new possibilities, new goals, and yes… more work.
Effort	Effort means sustained hard work. This is why it is so important to plan the effort with a group of solid supporters that will be ever-growing. A strong media advisory committee can share in this effort.
to Advance	To have advancement generally means to move in a certain direction, ostensibly with a goal somewhere in mind. If continuous effort is to be meaningful, it will have to be aimed at something. In order for this to be a goal developed and supported by a group of people, they will have to understand the library program.
the Library Program	Can you define the library program? Do supporters understand that it is more then just the room called the library, with the visible collection of books and other resources? If you asked your strongest supporter and best friend what you mean when you say library program, what would the answer be?
Shared with a	To truly share, the sense of personal ownership must be subjugated for the greater good. It also means that information is freely given and interpreted. Circulation statistics/cost of materials and new programs supported must be publicized, not necessarily in a separate newsletter on a web page but should be included in already existing publications.
Developed Community of	A developed community is one that has, over time, brought their individual and varying perspectives into a loosely defined group that finds its strength in both its diversities and commonalities. Rather than seeing the stakeholders as separate and distinct groups, over time, will it be possible to see these as a community?
Supporters	The notion that everyone loves the library may be true, but not everyone can be counted on to support library initiatives in the face of other competing entities. Support means strength that can be counted on.

The phrase "no news is good news" is not applicable here. No news ... is not good news ... in terms of library budgets. Every element of the library media program that is presented to the budget committee should already be familiar to them from other types of advocacy strategies. The fact that there is an information skills curriculum, that the school library media specialist is the teacher of information skills, that strong library collections increase reading, and that flexible access is the desired structure for a library program—all of these should start a pattern of nodding heads as the information is presented.

The ALA Library Advocates Handbook (ALA, 2000) is a great resource for advocacy. It stresses the importance of a clear message, a consistent effort, and a strong advocacy plan. Remember that advocacy is not about a one-time issue. Advocacy is a planned, deliberate, and sustained effort to raise awareness of an issue or issues. With the foundation of a strong advocacy program, the budget presentation itself is just a confirmation and an opportunity for library media program support to be quantified. This means that information about the library program and what it means to the instructional life of the school and the learning patterns of students should be common knowledge to the teachers. This is a daunting task, since a commonly heard complaint from many school library media specialists is that other teachers, administrators, and parents do not understand the purpose of the school library media program in the school. This is very true, and almost universally so. We have to tell them.

Neither marketing nor public relations are identical to advocacy. Public relations is a one-way message that tells a library story. Marketing, on the other hand, works to identify potential customers, find out what they want and need, and then respond to those needs. Advocacy is more than both of those, and yet each of those. Public relations and marketing are a part of advocacy.

Gary Hartzell, from his perspective as a past school administrator, titles the problem "The Invisible School Librarian" (Hartzell, 1994). Nowhere is this more true than in the preparation of library budgets. Why does an invisible library need funding? If the needs are not visible, then it is understandable why little or no funding is given to the school library. Hartzell's book, *Building Influence for the School Librarian* (Hartzell, 1997), is an excellent resource for school library media specialists trying to make their needs visible to budget decision makers. Hartzell reviews strategies for the building level and beyond to increase awareness of the functions of school library media programs in the instructional life of the school.

School library media specialists gain influence when they inform the principal of what they are doing and how the library program is influencing student achievement. They gain influence when they assist teachers with resources and show themselves to be teaching peers by collaborating on projects. School library media specialists gain influence with parents when they speak to the parent teacher association about how to choose books for children, what Internet sites are healthy, and which TV shows and channels children would find informative and fun. School library media specialists gain influence by being actively involved in life beyond the library.

Why Me?

The time required for advocacy to work is daunting. Advocacy takes the school library media specialist out of the library, since advocacy is most successful when you go to where your potential advocates are, rather than forcing them to come to you.

The good news is that a lack of funding given to a school library is generally the result of ignorance about the program, not anger. Very few people in a school are actively against the library program. However, it is also true that apart from the school library media specialist, very few people are fighting for the library program. School library media specialists are in competition for the school district dollar. Walters (1992) points out the need to recognize your competitors and to work with them to achieve joint goals.

One example of this could be the establishment of classroom libraries. In some ways, this could be seen as taking money from the school library media collection. However, is there a way to use that initiative? Perhaps we can support a classroom library and can also suggest placing more materials in the school library media center collection, either as a repository to make sure that another copy of the title always exists or as a way to coordinate the selection of classroom materials.

The school may be moving from computer labs to computers in the classrooms. Yet it is unlikely that enough space exists in the classroom for a sufficient number of computers to be available for all students in the class. Certainly the library program could be seen as needing more computers for individual and whole class research and the development of class projects.

The school library media program in the school as described in *Information Power* has a strong mission, a clear sense of purpose, and stated roles and responsibilities for school libraries (AASL/AECT, 1998). Most of our leaders would agree that the school library media field is conceptually mature. We know the elements of a strong school library media program. We can correlate the best practices of the school library media program with the acknowledged best practices of education. The school library media program is a constructivist's dream, a laboratory for inquiry-based learning, and a workshop for alternative assessment methods.

Historically, school library media specialists have been reluctant to speak too strongly or to be too political. Our profession, the ultimate helper in the helping profession of librarianship, may be rooted too strongly in the support aspects to readily take on the strong leadership role. We may fear the conflict that will inevitably occur, as our needs will be in conflict with others.

Hartzell, in his presentations on advocacy, uses a quote on a slide that says "there's pain either way" (Hartzell, 2001). Either you will have the pain of no money and resentment in being ignored, or you can have the pain from guilt at having the library program receive the money it deserves. Which pain will you choose? Which would mean better instruction, more learning, and more lifelong achievement for students?

Advocacy means using a planning process of setting goals, developing objectives, identifying strengths and weaknesses, identifying allies, making action plans, and evaluating progress (Turner, 1997, p. 3). Advocacy is not a bandwagon but is a carefully planned journey with a clear destination.

But why do we have to do this? Why can't teachers be taught to support the library program in their preparation programs? Why can't administrators be certified with an understanding of the importance of the library program in the school? Certainly those are goals. However, until those are achieved, we have to deal with what we have. We can't wait for the children in elementary school, who are benefiting from strong library programs, to grow up, become teachers, and them move into administration. We don't know how teachers, administrators, or parents developed their concepts of the school library media center. Supporters have to be trained, both overtly through presented information and covertly by modeling the role of the school library media program in the school.

Schement (2001) points out that although the school library media center can be known as the center of the school, and can even be open and accessible to all students, he sees that as a passive program. The library program he envisions can be a model of both equity and equality and of both giving all students the opportunity to succeed and then reaching out past the walls of the library program to ensure that all students do succeed.

Summary

James Hillman's book, *Kinds of Power* (1995), is an excellent book to read before beginning an advocacy program. In this book, Hillman reviews the language, the activities, and the stereotypes of power. He notes that the concept of "grow or die," of continually getting and acquiring more, inevitably leads to death and decay. Hillman, in his detailed analysis of the meaning of words, such as "office," "service," and "growth," gives us the meaning of power, one based on our ability to share our deepest beliefs and values, rather than to acquire things.

That is an analogy of the advocacy involved in school library media programs. Our efforts go toward fulfilling our mission. Our funding goals are based not on the things that we can acquire but on what those purchases will mean to others in the school.

The work of convincing decision makers in the school district community that th library program is worth supporting is advocacy. Putting a research-based budget together is a tremendous amount of work. A strong advocacy effect in conjunction with budget development gives energy to both processes.

STEP 1: MISSION AND BELIEFS

Review your statements of mission and beliefs. How are these articulated in the school? What would you like the interpretation to be? Write out your mission and beliefs in large letters and look at it as you work over a period of days. Now think of your school mission, important school issues, and issues of supporters and of the administrators? Where can your beliefs be found in the school? Look through written curriculum guides, statements from the principal, and all the paper that flows through your desk on a regular basis. Pay particular attention to those that caused you to wonder why you were not involved. With post-it notes or a computer program, such as Inspiration, make a mind-map of your beliefs, library goals, and other initiatives and where they fit in the school. What do you see as possible goals for the articulation of the library program with this other goals?

STEP 2: PRIORITIZE!

Look at your printed list of needs, goals, and issues articulated in the school. Most likely, you have found that the library program is "everywhere." Now look at where your priorities lie and where it seems that your priorities and the school priorities mesh. Color code these priorities so that you can see where you will concentrate your efforts.

STEP 3: WHY?

"Why" is a very powerful question? In this case, why should the administration, other teachers, parents, and the community care about your goals? The selfish, "What's in it for me?" must be answered from the administrator's perspective and the classroom teacher's perspective, in both a literal and figurative sense. As you look at the mind map of library program goals you have created, step into the shoes of the decision makers that you want to include among your supporters. Ask these questions from their points of view?

What's in this budget for me?

Why should I support the library program?

What will happen if I don't support the program?

Try to make your answers for each of these questions focus on instructional goals, not emotional ones. If you were one of them, would you vote for your budget over other goals?

What Would Savvy School Library Media Specialists Do?

Savvy school library media specialists advocate every day, all the time. They celebrate National Library Week with enthusiasm. They use library stationery and library stickers and have business cards.

Savvy school library media specialists see themselves as managing the program, but they know the program is owned by the users. They ask for feedback and suggestions from students, teachers, parents, and administrators. They develop functional media advisory committees and use them to assist with program decisions.

Chapter 5

How Much Money is Needed?

It would be nice if planning the school library media program were as simple as following a recipe to make a cake. Take 10,000 books, add 15 computers, spice things up with pinches and handfuls of other equipment and materials, stir with one full-time library media specialist and one full-time clerical assistant and bake in the warm support of teachers, parents, and administrators for many happy years to come.

Unfortunately, it's just not that easy.

What does a library program need, and how much does it cost? These extremely important questions are very difficult to answer. Economists refer to this dilemma as "funding adequacy." Briefly mentioned in Chapter 3 of this book, funding adequacy is defined as the minimum amount of money needed to produce a product or service. As we discussed, this is a much easier concept in manufacturing than it is in education.

In business, it may be very easy to cost out the elements and processes needed to make each cookie in the package. The company managers can determine the relative cost of both regular or double-stuff fillings, can decide which market strategy will make the public believe that it can't live without this particular type of cookie, and can decide whether the relative cost of inputs over outputs will produce enough of a profit to keep company stockholders happy. Manufacturers constantly search for ways to reduce the cost of inputs or to streamline the manufacturing process in order to maximize outputs.

In education, it is not so easy. The outspoken frustration of business people in the taxpaying community or on the school board reflects the input-output mindset. They may claim that educators concentrate on outputs with no thought to the cost of inputs, and in some respects, that is true. There may be screams of frustration when no administrator present at a public meeting can give estimates as to the educational impact of a new instructional program on test scores or other outputs. The arguments that used to be valid, describing the planned use and the student need, are no longer sufficient. Taxpayers now want to know how much test scores will increase, how this will save money, and other statistics that are difficult and almost impossible to estimate. No amount of testing, screening, or other kinds of elements can tell educators exactly which educational processes to apply to each five-year-old who enters the kindergarten door. Even if we knew the exact educational remedy to apply to every situation, we would not be able to even guess how long it would take, how much it would cost, or how effective it would be. We cannot predict the success of each educational procedure, the developmental rate of each child, or predict the now-unknown factors that, in the future, will affect each of these.

How much will it cost to educate one person? In truth, we have no idea. In the same way, in the library media program, we do not know what it takes to achieve our mission to "ensure that students and staff are effective users of ideas and information" (AASL/AECT, 1998, p. 6). In order to even hazard a guess, we would have to have a reliable definition of what a school library program with the mission achieved is like, not only in description of activities or behaviors, but also in terms of quantities of resources, uses, and user actions. We would then have to be able to assess each person's initial level of "lifelong learning score" and be able to chart progress along the way.

All schools do not have exactly the same population, and each school's students have unique learning needs. Refer to the graphic in Figure 5.1 of the school library media production function. As before, we see the inputs of resources, staff, collections, and money. Remember also the discussion in Chapter 3 on filters. When the manufacturing process is held up by a glitch in the stream of inputs, or an error in manufacturing, it has to be fixed via a filter of some sort. If the chocolate chips turn out to be less sweet than usual, the cookie company may decide to add sugar to the recipe. This adds cost, but it may be cheaper than finding another source for chocolate. In education, we have filters as well, but finding another source, i.e., another group of students, is not an option. We have to add processes, resources, and services to create the "fix" or the needed filter.

Figure 5.1: School Library Media Production Function

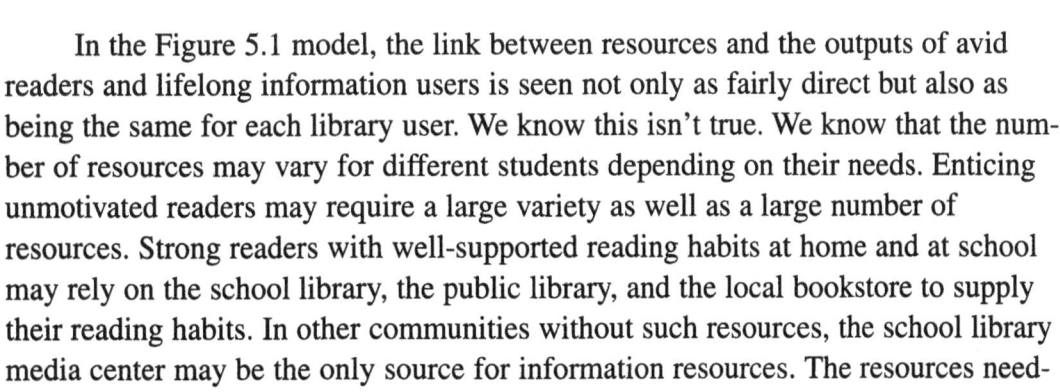

In the Figure 5.1 model, the link between resources and the outputs of avid readers and lifelong information users is seen not only as fairly direct but also as being the same for each library user. We know this isn't true. We know that the number of resources may vary for different students depending on their needs. Enticing unmotivated readers may require a large variety as well as a large number of resources. Strong readers with well-supported reading habits at home and at school may rely on the school library, the public library, and the local bookstore to supply their reading habits. In other communities without such resources, the school library media center may be the only source for information resources. The resources needed for the school library media production function for each school library media program are very different.

Sometimes school library media specialists speculate that it would be easier to dump all the resources and technology from the library program and start over. Even if your collection is beyond hope, you most likely have to start with what you have and have to build on that. You may have an extremely old collection, and your budget over the last several years may have been insignificant. This is an important reason for implementing a filter (a process that improves raw materials). Outdated equipment, a cramped facility, and other limiting factors also require a filter. You don't have the raw materials you need, and you need to change the funding process in order to minimize the impact these sub-standard materials have on the children.

It is very important in budget requests to keep these extra considerations for your students in the mind of the budget decision makers. Start with a list similar to the chart in Figure 5.2 and list why your library program needs more money than other libraries. In other words, what educational filters (aside from the filter necessary for replacing outdated materials) are in place for your student population? For instance, you may have a large number of children speaking languages other than English or a highly diverse population. What are the reasons why your school library media program needs to have more resources than the "average" program? Are the children in your school reading extremely below or extremely above reading level for their age group?

Remember that the lack of diversity in a school is an equally strong incentive for a highly diverse collection as the more diverse school. In a non-diverse school, how else will children see and recognize the multicultural world they will live in as adults except through books and information resources? The need for representing diversity may be greatest in schools that are not highly diverse. In this way, children in the Beaver Cleaver Middle School can at least come to know, through books and other resources if not through personal experiences, that it is important to understand and to accept children not like themselves.

Look carefully at the Figure 5.2 and enter data about your school.

Figure 5.2: Filters at the School Level

Why is your school different from other schools? Why do you need more materials/resources?

What is the impact of your identified needs? What specific materials and resources do you need?

What will be the positive effects on student learning if these needs are satisfied and your requests for resources are granted?

What is the negative impact if your requests are not granted?

Our inability to state the level of funding adequacy for library media programs is a major dilemma. In a realistic economic climate, educators have to present their budgets to business people, who expect business principles to be applied. Legislators sometimes seem only to be concerned about test scores, rather than the welfare of the children.

A discussion of filters, of making education equitable for all students, and of presenting logical solutions to educational challenges is rarely presented in budget terms. However, for many children, becoming lifelong learners, effective information users, and avid readers is the only path to success, and that path lies through the school library media program. If we are to accomplish our mission, we must have adequate resources to support the services of the library program.

It is the responsibility of the school library media specialist to articulate budget needs in such a way that the budget decision makers in the school can understand and can support those goals. Being able to justify budget requests is an important step. We will begin with regional accrediting bodies and will then move through the standards, past and present, that make up what are generally considered to be the resources needed by school library media programs.

Mandates and Standards

The favorite lament of superintendents, and deservedly so, is that of unfunded mandates. Unfunded mandates refer to the laws and regulations that specify what school districts are required to offer, with no requisite specified funding source. The intense lobbying effort against unfunded mandates is one of the major obstacles to laws requiring all schools to have school library media professionals and support staff in each state.

For that reason, "they say we have to have" sentences usually provoke defensive responses by school administration. It is far better to evoke comparisons. Recommendations are easier to swallow than mandates, even though in rough budget times, mandates are more likely to be funded. Getting people to listen at this stage is extremely important. Once the seed for program support is planted, and there is agreement on the goals, implementation is never far behind.

School districts are more likely to want to offer the same programs and services as neighboring school districts do. This is an excellent strategy to use with the local community. The value of real estate is sometimes dependent on the perceived quality of the schools. Keeping up with the Jones School can be a very strong tool. Visit other library programs, especially those with excellent facilities or interesting programs. The state school library media conference is an excellent way to network with other school library media specialists.

Quantitative standards are always under debate in the field. The standard of "one new book per pupil per year" from the 1960 Standards for School Library Media Programs is still used as a goal for the funding of resources (AASL/AECT, 1960), although that has been very difficult to achieve. In the 1975 national standards—*Media Programs; District and School*—quantitative standards for every aspect of the school library media program were developed for library media specialists to be able to say how many, how much, and which items should be in a library media center (AASL/AECT, 1975).

In some ways, any set of qualitative standards, being set in time, cannot take into account changing technologies and will become quickly outdated at a time of rapidly changing technology. The 1986 *Information Power* moved away from the quantitative guidelines to more qualitative guidelines, noting the elements that each program should have as outcomes, rather than inputs (AASL/AECT, 1986).

In the latest revision of *Information Power*, qualitative has merged with quantitative to list some things that each area should have. Although these are not as strong as some would wish, remember the concept of funding adequacy. It is very difficult to establish one recipe for every student in every school. Advocacy fills in the gaps to explain national standards to our audience. Figure 5.3 shows the evolution of the move from quantitative national standards to more qualitative guidelines and recommendations.

Figure 5.3: Comparison Chart of National Guidelines

	1960	1975	1986	1998
Size of main library room	10% of the student body x 35 square feet per student	15-30% of enrollment x 40 square feet per student	Used comparative survey data to show the collection sizes in elementary, middle, and high school high-service programs.	Little to no numeric standards given
Magazines	25-120	50-175		
Books	10 books per student	16-24 per user (includes all print formats)		
Audiovisuals	Depends on use	Specific numeric standards given for each type		
Overhead Projector (as an example of equipment)	1 per building	1 for every 50 users (including students)		

Figure 5.3 shows that, over time, the very specific guidelines have given way to more general standards based not on ownership but on student outcomes. Although it is true that *Information Power* does not have the numeric "have to have" data, it does paint a strong picture of the vision that can become a reality in a strong library program. School library media specialists need to apply that vision to their particular schools and need to then recreate the school library media production function according to those needs. The move away from specific quantitative numeric inputs to program outcomes is not only seen in our national standards but in others as well. Starting from the outcomes, then working backwards to design the program, and then establishing a statement of need for resources creates a strong budget defense.

Regional Accreditation Associations

Apart from national guidelines, regional accrediting bodies also have established program standards. Although there are districts that do not engage in the regional accreditation process, most schools are at least aware of the importance of these and strive to at least come close to meeting the standard. Figure 5.4 offers a comparison of each of the major accreditation bodies. There are some schools and school districts that choose not to be evaluated by the regional accrediting body. This does not mean that those standards do not have some power in the district. Even if your school or school district does not engage in the accrediting process, it can still be argued that the school library media program should be of the same quality as surrounding schools.

Figure 5.4 compares standards from the Southern Association of Colleges and Schools (SACS), the New England Association of Schools and Colleges (NEASC), and the North Central Association Commission on Accreditation and School Improvement (NCACASI).

Figure 5.4:	Sample Comparison of Regional Accreditation Standards		
	SACS	**NEASC**	**NCACASI**
	Includes current technological formats	Adequate space	Balance of print, nonprint, and electronic resources
	Current, comprehensive, and carefully selected	Appropriate, supportive of curriculum, accessible to students, and reflective of global and multicultural society	Sufficient resources are budgeted and spent annually to maintain a current collection
	10 books per students	Adequately maintained, cataloged, and updated	Provision is made for replacing and updating materials
	Southern Association of Colleges and Schools www.sacs.org	New England Association of Schools and Colleges www.neasc.org	North Central Association Commission on Accreditation and School Improvement. www.ncacasi.org

The qualitative elements of each of these standards must be taken into account just as much as the quantitative ones. For instance, in the SACS standards, the element most often used to evaluate library collections is the standard of 10 books per student. That standard, and others like it, has garnered much criticism. It has prevented some library media specialists from weeding out unwanted and outdated materials, since they were ordered to make sure that the collection did not fall below the standard of 10 books per student.

However, a closer look at the SACS standard also reveals a qualitative element to the standard. The amount required for each school is not just 10 volumes but 10 usable volumes that are current, comprehensive, and carefully selected. Therefore, the only books that should be counted for each library are the ones that are usable. Books that should have been weeded, but have not been, should not be counted to the standard. The New England Association of Schools and Colleges and the North Central Association Commission on Accreditation and School Improvement also include language in their standards that requires current resources in library media collections. Note that NEASC requires adequate space for the library media center. NCACASI stresses weeding out and replacing materials.

It is important that school library media specialists be able to interpret the meaning of these standards for administration. Principals may need to be reminded that school library media specialists who may visit the school on an accreditation team will instantly recognize a substandard collection. It sometimes helps to point

Chapter 5: How Much Money is Needed?

out that the library collection will be cited as a weakness either way. It may be the principal's choice as to whether the collection will be cited for being small, but praised for being well-weeded and for containing current and usable resources, or whether the collection will be cited for containing inadequate resources, for being old, outdated, and in need of weeding, and for still not containing the required number of usable resources.

If presented and explained in terms of how the collection will be viewed by a visiting library-media-trained visitor, the principal may decide that weeding would be the preferable option. Sometimes it helps to have a neighboring library media specialist visit to give impressions of the collection.

State Standards

Each state may also have some regulations or guidelines as to what a school library media center should contain. Remember to check not only your state standards but also surrounding states. It's important to note how your school compares with excellence in the field, wherever that is located. Most state standards will be entirely qualitative, without any specific numeric value listed. Again, it is up to the library media specialist to evaluate the program according to the available standards and to then interpret that evaluation for the faculty and staff. You may find that there is more interest in improving the library media center collection and services than you thought.

Beyond the Standards

The problem with all standards, including the aforementioned, is that they do not cover the breadth and the complexity of a library program. Regional accreditation tends to cover only books and to mention or hint at technology briefly. Other standards may mention some electronic resources but not nearly to the depth that a library media program should have. State standards sometimes only cover what is funded, although there are many instances that go beyond the specifics in the regulation of what is covered. No one single standard adequately covers the variety of materials, resources, and programs needed for the modern school library.

Our best sources for the needs of the library media program are two-fold. *Information Power*, the national guidelines of the American Association of School Librarians, gives us the basics of what is needed for a library media program. The other resource comes from the research in the field. "Library Power," the grant-funded school library media enhancement program in the 1980s and early 1990s, has greatly added to this research by creating models of strong school library media programs and by documenting the instructional impact of those programs (Zweizig & Hopkins, 1999).

Between *Information Power* and the "Library Power" research, we can draw the important inputs, processes, and outcomes for the library media program in your school.

Staff

Minimum acceptable staffing for a library media center program is generally considered to be one full-time, certified professional library media specialist and one full-time, clerical assistant per school. The justification for this minimal staffing is outlined in the AASL position paper on staffing <www.ala.org/aasl>. For schools with larger enrollment (usually approaching 1,000), more than one professional and one clerical assistant will be needed.

Non-funded positions in a typical school library also include parent volunteers and student assistant positions. Although these people do not require taxpayer-based salaries, they should also be listed in budget discussions. One reason to do this is it shows you are doing your part to find ways to execute the duties required in a school library without additional funding. In some ways, soliciting volunteer support is similar to listing in-kind contributions on a grant application. It adds to the value of the program, while not soliciting additional funding.

Student assistants and parent volunteers can be an additional cost item, however. It takes staff time to recruit, to train, and to thank volunteers. Generally, the use of parent volunteers and student assistants is seen as a positive activity by administration and is therefore a program outcome. It gets parents into the school where they can be of assistance, and it gives students a sense of pride and ownership. In a performance-based budget, for example, staff time and any resources needed to facilitate the volunteer program must be included in the accounting and rationale.

Any activities that are tied to the parent- or student-volunteer process should be quantified if possible. A "thank-you" tea for parents at the end of the school year should be included in the budget. Sending flyers home, even if the paper comes from the office, and giving student assistants some type of gift at the end of the year, even if the cost is just pennies, need to be noted. Some library media specialists will note that these funds come out of their own personal pockets, rather than school district coffers. That may not change, but at least the administration and school peers will see the amount that you are spending, and you will have a clearer picture of how much it costs to run the school library media program. It is important to present these figures without whining or asking for reimbursement. This is simply a cost-analysis of the functions of the school library media program from a budget perspective. It is not an opportunity to show your martyred, self-less dedication to the children of the district.

Many grant funding applications require the use of matching funds. It makes sense in the budget request for staffing to show the matching funds that you provide to support the total staffing of the school library media programs, both in terms of non-funded positions and for your time in recruiting, training, and organizing staff members.

Facilities

Facilities are one of the few areas in the library media center program that are clearly spelled out in standards. Your state standards should have a complete and detailed list of specifications for what goes in a school library media center, and there are several excellent books on the topic as well. Klasing (1991) and Anderson (1990) are commonly used for a basic overview.

There are three types of activities that must occur simultaneously in the library media center program. First, there should be a place for large group instruction. For larger schools, at least two areas must be included, even if one area is a story corner or a space for a floor activity. Second, while the large group instruction is being conducted, there should be individual tables for small groups to gather and to work independently or under the casual supervision of an adult. The small group tables should be close enough to the large group instruction area that they are visible to the library media specialist, but not so close enough that they are distracting.

Finally, the room must be large enough so that while there is a large group being taught and there are small groups working, individual students may come in and browse the shelves without disturbing either of the previously mentioned activities. This means that tables should not be pushed close to the shelves. Students should be able to browse the collection without being targets for taps, pushes, or comments by other children.

Notice that in the description of what must occur simultaneously, square footage was not mentioned, and it probably should be minimized in a budget request. To homeowners, a 3,000 square foot library may evoke a comparison to the square footage of an extremely expensive house. It is much more effective to visualize the activities that have to occur in the library than to think about empty square footage.

Remember, also, that the library media center does not start at the door of the library room. Start with the front door of the school. Do visitors to the school know that there is a library in the school? Do they know where it is? Walk to the library from the main office, keeping an eye out for signage along the way. What signs or displays on the outside of the library doors give enticing hints as to what happens inside?

Most facilities standards only talk about the nuts and bolts of the library… how many books, tables, chairs, and so on. Facilities are more than books and mortar. How inviting is the library media center? For elementary schools, is the story corner inviting and colorful? Are the displays and the shelves arranged in such a way that students are tempted to browse? For secondary schools, does the leisure reading area's definition of comfortable seating remind you of a dentist's office? Waiting room furniture is not going to be an invitation to lounge and read for middle- and high-school students.

Finally, evaluate the "stuff" in the room itself. Don't forget items, such as a telephone and the teaching area. Make a wish list of what you need on the Figure 5.5, which is found later in this chapter. Include renovations to the electrical wiring that you need, new drapes or carpet, or other material.

Collection

The book collection is the most visible part of the services of the library program. Even after 50 years of the inclusion of audiovisual materials into libraries, they still are hidden away in back rooms. A patron wanting all resources on the Civil War may have to go into four or five different areas, some of which are under lock and key, to retrieve the resources. It would be easier to analyze collections if we shelved by information, rather than by format. Still, when presenting budget requests for materials, it is important to mention all formats, especially since some of these may not be visible.

It is important to have a factual basis for making a recommendation on the changes needed in the collection. For that reason, a thorough analysis of the existing collection should be conducted. There are many ways to conduct a collection analysis, and some consultants are readily available to provide their services. A simple method used in graduate school classes is outlined in the "Collection Analysis Procedure" section of this chapter. For a method that will show statistical significance, Doll and Barron's (2002) book, *Managing and Analyzing Your Collection* listed in the Bibliography of this book, outlines an easy method that is more in-depth, but that still can be easily performed by the school library media specialist.

One of the more popular outcomes of collection analysis techniques is to establish an average age of the collection. Although highly touted, take caution against such a statistic. The average age is meaningless to your purposes, yet it is extremely valuable to your budget opponents. We need to be very careful about presenting a perfect weapon to use against us to those who wish to punch holes in our carefully constructed budget justification.

An average date of 1973, for example, may create some "oohs" and "ahs" from the audience. However, the first person who stands up and argues that of course it is old because there are many classics in the collection will give others pause. Most people of midlife and older simply do not consider the 1970s or the 1980s to be old. Pointing out that of course the library has fairy tales, many works of a classical author such as Dickens, or historical works further weakens the argument. Although each of these can be refuted, they must be done individually and only to a limited extent. Once a reason for not supporting the budget request is lodged in the mind of detractors, it will not be dislodged.

It is much better to give the percent of collection in decades. The copyright date of 1973 may or may not seem to be old. However, stating that 70% of the collection is more than 20 years old, although it may average out to the same statistic of 1973, is irrefutable. Regardless of the number of classics or historical works, most people would instantly agree that more than 10—20% of the collection should be within the same range as the children who will be reading these books.

The statistic of an average copyright age for a collection is so fraught with misinterpretation, and the chance that it could be used in opposition to a budget defense is so apparent, it is best simply to avoid it. Remember that for many people, "old" is before they graduated from high school. The year 1974 is of course far too old as an average age, but to some people, it was their senior year in high school, and just yesterday they were having their children in the 1980s. Rather than convince them of why that date is old, it is easier and less debatable to point out that only 5% of the collection used to support the science curriculum has been copyrighted within the last 10 years.

Although there are some automated catalogs that will perform analyses of the collection copyright dates to give some indication of the collection age, the simple hands-on procedure outlined in the "Collection Analysis Procedure" section of this chapter will allow the school library media specialist to give context to the statistics by describing the shelves and the condition of the books and by giving examples. Although when used at the district level it ensures an equal sampling of the same number of books regardless of size, the Doll and Barron (2002) book uses a method that accounts for collection size.

Collection analysis takes a great deal of time. One should expect to spend about seven to 10 hours performing the data collection, and probably about another five to seven hours analyzing the data. The analysis outline also recommends looking in-depth at only two curriculum areas. Further work in more subject areas would most likely indicate the same conclusions, however, some school librarians try to outline the resources available in each major curriculum area.

Collection Analysis Procedure

Note, this method was devised for graduate school classes. It was designed to be fair for all students in the class, regardless of grade level, size of school, or size of collection.

Step 1: Sample 20 Books on 20 Shelves

Count the total number of shelves in the library collection. Divide the number of shelves by 20 (180 shelves divided by 20 = nine). Starting at a random shelf in the collection, look at the first 20 books and note the information from Step 2. To choose the next shelf to sample, count the shelves by the number you found as a result of the formula above (in this case, nine) and look at the first 20 books on that shelf. Continue through the collection.

Step 2: Record the Data

Use the chart similar to the one presented on the next page to record data that you found about each book. Most recent circulation is always interesting, but that may be difficult to tell. Condition can be described as good, fair, or poor.

Call Number	Copyright Date	Condition of the Book	Recent Use

Step 3: Charts and Graphs

Use the chart function on the spreadsheet to produce charts and graphs showing the percent of the collection copyrighted in each decade.

Remember again to resist the temptation to calculate and present average age. It detracts from the strength of your presentation and presents opportunities for the presentation to be criticized. Rather than explaining that "of course, we have a large number of classics," it is far stronger to present the percentage of the collection copyrighted in the last decade, especially for the nonfiction. A "yes, but" presentation sounds weak and defensive.

You can go further with the collection analysis and choose two curriculum areas for in-depth study of the books in those areas. Choose one subject area from the science curriculum and another from social sciences. Be sure to link the topic with the specific curriculum objective from the state curriculum guidelines. It is very powerful to be able to state that this is a required subject for all students in this grade level, and we have only "x" number of books and have only a small percentage copyrighted in the last five years. Look at all the books that you have on that topic (it should be a topic narrow enough that there are fewer than 20 books) and present the same previously mentioned charts and graphs. If there is a problem with depth and timeliness, it will be revealed.

After the collection analysis, a weeding plan will have to be developed. With the two curriculum areas, determine how many of those books are truly usable, in accordance with the regional curriculum guidelines. Extrapolate that to the rest of the collection. The same procedure can be conducted with other elements of the collection, such as the audiovisual collection.

With each school's instructional needs being so different, it is difficult to present information on needed collection size. You are attempting to identify funding adequacy, how many resources you need to educate your students. This is very difficult, as we previously discussed. However, remember as well that an estimate based on your previous research will help your audience determine quickly how close your collection is to the standard. Use the chart in Figure 5.5 as a model only. You may decide to subdivide that chart, highlight different areas, or use different parts of the collection.

Figure 5.5: Budget Needs

Inputs	Present	Standard	Excellence
	Existing collection of current and usable resources	Figures from state, regional, or national comparison	Based on your application of the school library media production function
Books			
Audiovisuals			
Facilities			
Equipment			
Staff			
Electronic Resources			
Other Types of Access			
Other Materials			

Figure 5.5 will take some time to evolve. In the column labeled "Present," you will need to establish the number of resources that are usable. You will not count items simply taking up space on the shelf. For some categories, such as staff or facilities, you may want to either include a number, such as square feet or the number of

staff (1:1, for one professional and one assistant), or a descriptive word such as "adequate."

In the next column, you should identify the standard that you will be using for each box. It may be easiest to develop a code for the regional, the state, or the national standards you are using. It is acceptable to use national comparison figures for those areas in which there are no standards. You must base your estimate of what is needed on more than just a number plucked from the air. You will be asked to identify the source of your information. Your own research may be seen as more applicable to the local collection than national standards.

Remember that the "Standard" column indicates funding adequacy. It is "standard," not excellence. Your own drawings of the school library media production function and what filters are needed in your school, as well as the local, the state, the regional, and the national standards are used to develop that number for each column. It may seem incredibly high to you. However, remember that you can support each number with sound research of the field and your own action research.

The last column is the drive for excellence. Remember the earlier discussion on the need for equity of educational outcomes. What if each child really could achieve the mission statement of the school and district? How many resources would you need to support that effort? Find the library programs from your previous research with the resources you would like to emulate. Place those numbers in the column marked "Excellence."

Books

The generally accepted minimum number of books in a collection is 10 books per student, or a minimum collection of 6,000—8,000 volumes. Electronic resources, no matter what the number, will not diminish this requirement. Electronic resources may affect the size of the reference collection and may reduce the need for print encyclopedias and other expensive reference books. Electronic resources can also affect the number of magazines ordered for research use. However, the basic circulating book collection will not be affected tremendously. Electronic resources have added to the number of resources students may use, however, they have not reduced the number of materials required for basic research. Electronic resources, Internet use, and television watching may be vying for a student's leisure time, but they have not reduced the need for the leisure reading of fiction books.

Establish a loss rate as well. You should know, by circulation and by the last several inventories, the number of books lost or missing each year. Remember that if you are paid for lost books, that money should be used to purchase new copies of the title or a replacement title. If you are seeking additional budget funds for a high loss rate, it will be difficult to justify receiving replacement money as well as additional funding. It may be considered double-dipping.

Enter the number of books that you will need to bring the collection up to standard and then up to excellence. Then enter the number of books that need to be purchased each year to maintain that level. Remember to take into account any changes in curriculum or in population that may affect the collection. New curriculum and any redistricting of the school will cause changes in the collection as it reflects the school, its curriculum, and the school community. If there is a cycle of curriculum revision, it may be possible to add to the annual amount to purchase new materials required for the curriculum changes.

Audiovisuals

Either you have a small collection of audiovisual materials at the school, or students and staff have access to a large collection of audiovisual materials housed at a district or regional location. Regardless, access to audiovisual materials needs to be identified in the budget request. Just like non-cost, personnel items, such as volunteer hours, non-cost access to other collections needs to be identified. The audiovisual collection at the regional or state lending library may not be a cost-factor for your budget or even for your school district budget, but someone pays for it at some level. It is very helpful to note these free-to-you types of services at all levels. This is not limited to just audiovisual materials but should be included for all types of materials, including cable or satellite television services.

Unfortunately, there is little research-based data to describe the optimal collection size or the diversity of format in the area of audiovisuals. Surveys can be of assistance to find what types of materials are desired, since most audiovisual needs depend on individual teaching styles and children's learning styles. A comprehensive survey conducted every several years can be of assistance over the long term. However, faculty turnover has more of an effect in this area than any other part of the collection. One new staff member can turn a specific area in the audiovisual collection from being fairly adequate to being inadequate or from being used constantly to not being used at all.

When counting the initial collection, you must only count materials that are used or that are usable. The several hundred captioned filmstrips that are of no value to the teaching or learning processes should not be included and should be weeded.

Equipment

From anecdotal evidence, it should be apparent what materials are needed for the collection in the area of equipment. Teachers are probably most vocal about needed equipment, especially when it has been lacking for some time. VCRs, TVs, and other audiovisual equipment needs can be noted, with estimations of the number needed based on teacher complaints. However, do not ignore new types of equipment that may be unknown to the teachers. Information gleaned at conferences or picked up from professional reading on new types of technology to make student learning deeper, faster, or better should be presented to the faculty.

Student access to audiovisual materials may be important as well. A combination TV/VCR near the collection of college videos may be a new addition to the equipment collection but would add value to the college and career collection. Even though it seems obvious, you may have to make explicit to your audience that the purpose of equipment is to make use of the resources. Without adequate equipment, the resources will not be used.

Other Materials

Library supplies, materials for decorations, and signage are sometimes dismissed as relatively unimportant when compared with materials directly used by students and teachers. It is important, however, to consider the needs for each item. Think of items that would increase the value to the collection by increasing use.

Travel, although paid for by the district or school (or not), is important to note as well. Certainly travel to the state library conference is expected and should be listed. The AASL biannual national conference may be one that can be noted as well as conferences for other national associations. This is especially important if you pay for these items yourself, as many in the field do. After each conference, it is appropriate to thank the school and the district for allowing you the time to attend. In these reports, you should note learning events that you attended, conversations of value that gave you insight into the programs, and other occurrences that have added value to the library program in your school. Revisit these reports and note implications for the library media budget.

Review Figure 5.5 after completion to make sure you have covered all the instructional inputs for the school library media program; it is a necessary step for this process. You may find that you need to keep changing the structure of the rows and columns as you identify more areas that apply to your specific schools. You should add enough categories to accurately portray the library media program in your school and district. Does the chart, when completed, represent everything that happens in the program and everything that you as library media specialist do?

Summary

Look over the finished analysis of budget needs. At this point, you do not have any costs associated with each of these items, but you should have a rough draft of your budget needs. In some ways, many school library media specialists begin the budgeting process backwards. They begin with the amount available to them and then work backwards to decide how they will spend it. That is less budgeting and more simple accounting. The first step is to decide what you need, and a careful review of the elements of this chapter has shown you that. In the next chapter, we will review the costs associated with each element and will go forward to develop a budgeting plan.

Starting thinking about the justification of excellence as we move through the next chapters. In many districts, school boards and superintendents constantly present the budget as "bare bones," because of a perceived need to show the extreme cost-consciousness of the district. In order to follow that lead, you will need to be preparing arguments along that line as well, and at the same time, you will be outlining the path to excellence for school library media programming.

For You TO DO

Show off. Learn how to use the charts/graphs features of your favorite spreadsheet program. Embed tidbits of information that you gleaned from doing the collection analysis procedure into library newsletters. Take data from the School Report Card and tie it to data that you have, such as circulation. With charts and graphs, a picture truly is worth a thousand words.

What Would Savvy School Library Media Specialists Do?

Savvy school library media specialists know that a little information a little bit at a time is better than a lot of completely new information. Savvy school librarians share each new tidbit they find as they find it, so that the story unfolds for everyone involved at the same time.

Savvy school library media specialists use charts and graphs, rather than pages of text. If a picture is worth a thousand words, then a well-labeled and concise graph is worth well more than a thousand. Learn how to use a spreadsheet and share the knowledge of what you find.

Savvy school library media specialists know that they have to be excited before anyone else will stir out of complacency. Savvy school library media specialists are thrilled with the research that they find, and they eagerly share.

Savvy school library media specialists know that time is precious and that back room administrative tasks take time away from teaching and learning. Savvy school library media specialists seek collaborative opportunities with the basic math and computer applications classes to do the research for them.

Chapter 6

Adding Dollars to the Budget Picture

Picture yourself presenting your carefully researched library media program needs to a budget committee. Everything is going smoothly, until someone looks and snarls ... "Sounds wonderful, but how much will all of this cost?" Previous to this chapter, we have only discussed budget needs, with no thought to how much things cost. There is a valid reason for allowing the budget development process to unfold in this way.

The initial process of gathering dusty data and doing the calculations to form a picture of the budget history of the district takes hours. Spending time analyzing collections, surveying parents, students, and teachers, and developing and implementing advocacy plans take equally long. Many school library media specialists find this process tedious and not worth the time spent. Some may think there is no way the school district will ever decide to add any money to the school library media budget let alone choose to make the library program a budget priority.

Having your budget request denied by the school board or administration can be disheartening. However, not presenting the budget because of the fear of being denied is illogical and takes the concept of the self-fulfilling prophecy to a new low. It also comes very close to being considered negligent of job responsibilities.

Although there may be times that budget requests will be turned down by the school board, it is its job to consider carefully all requests that will positively impact student learning. It is the job of the school library media specialist to thoughtfully present carefully-researched budget requests. If needs are never presented, there is no chance they will ever be funded. Regardless of how low the chance of budget presentation success may be, it is certainly greater than if the requests were never made. If the budget development process started with a look at how much money is needed, chances are the sheer size of the budget figure would create an unwillingness to take the process further.

The processes outlined in this chapter are fuzzy. Options are presented for a variety of ways to arrive at a final budget figure for each expenditure category. In the work up to this point, careful steps were prepared to gather data for each page of the budget presentation. This chapter relies more on subjective professional judgment. Because of the previously discussed problems with funding adequacy, much of the data in this chapter should be based on your own specific school and the existing collection.

To begin, refer back to the Figure 4.1: What Does Your School District Value? in Chapter 4 for your list of new programs and major budget implications for other programs. Keep remembering that the only criteria that makes the library media program absent from that list is a well-constructed plan for student learning improvement that involves the library media center program. True, by the end of this chapter, we will be making decisions as to how much money to request, based on the school district's fiscal capacity, area economics, and the economic climate of the district. But before that can happen, before the small pieces of the picture can be presented, the budget audience should have a sense of the big picture.

You have already achieved much of that big picture with your work thus far. This chapter will help you reduce those budget needs to budget dollars. In working with Figure 6.1, you should use the budget needs you adapted from Figure 5.5 in Chapter 5. Remember that with needed adaptations, your worksheet may look slightly different.

Figure 6.1: Budget Worksheet

Inputs	Recommended to Bring to Standard	Year One	Year Two	Year Three
Books				
Audiovisuals				
Facilities				
Equipment				
Staff				
Electronic Resources				
Other Types of Access				
Other Materials				

In the first column, we will place the dollar amount that is needed to bring the collection up to standard. Then, in the ensuing columns, we will bring the amount recommended to maintain that standard. You may want to keep the spreadsheet based on Figure 5.5 open as you work through this chapter. It may even be helpful to combine the spreadsheets to develop one that makes the best sense for your collection.

After completing the work in Chapter 5, you should have a good idea of the recommended needs for your library. Work through the next sections to find the amount to place in each of the areas. This will give a good estimate of the amount needed.

Gathering Financial Data

Up to this point, you have made notes and have collected data on the collection. Now, you need to gather financial data. Although the average price of a library book is reported data in several national publications, such as *School Library Journal, Publishers' Weekly*, and the *Bowker Annual*, there may be some in your audience who will question the accuracy of that statistic. National data is sometimes easy to dismiss, since there may be a valid reason why your community and your school are different. Perhaps you buy large quantities of paperbacks. Maybe you have dropped some more expensive magazine subscriptions in favor of electronic research tools. Perhaps there is a large district library of audiovisuals that meet each teacher's needs. Regardless, you now need the average price for materials that you spend.

If you are new to the position as school library media specialist, you may have difficulty finding out what was spent in the library media center. Read through your files to total what was spent for books and other categories of funding for the last two years. Be warned that it is not unusual for a new school library media specialist to find no record that any money has been spent on the school library media center. While it is possible that no materials have been purchased for the collection, it is unlikely. Check with the building secretary or the district purchasing office to see if you can find more information.

Look at Figure 6.2 and complete it to find the average price for materials following the procedures outlined. You may have to adapt Figure 6.2 as needed to suit your collection, your resources, and your budget needs. Remember not to make the chart too detailed. It takes less than a minute to lose people with short attention spans, and nothing does that quicker than droning through columns of numbers.

Figure 6.2: Finding the Average Price per Item for Library Materials

	Year One			Year Two			Two-Year Average
	Number Purchased	Amount Spent	Average Spent per Item	Number Purchased	Amount Spent	Average Spent per Item	
Books							
Audiovisuals							
Facilities							
Equipment							
Electronic Resources							
Other Types of Access							
Other Materials							

With the directions that follow, fill in the amounts in Figure 6.2. Using the last two years of library media expenditure data, record the total number of items purchased and the total amount spent. Divide to find the average amount spent per item. Do the same for the second year and then average the amount spent over the last two years. To be completely accurate, you can use the inflation calculator to bring each amount up to current dollar levels, in the same way we used it in Chapter 2. However, the cost of living increase over the past several years has been very small, and the difference would have been pennies.

Books

In order to perform this calculation, you first will need to decide on your definition of a "book." Are you going to include in that definition all resources in book form, including paperbacks as well as reference, professional, and other resources? There are good reasons for making such a decision. Eliminating reference books takes away the decisions of how to deal with expensive sets of books. You may want to figure reference as a separate category, showing how materials for research are much more expensive than books for the collection. This might also be a way to justify the purchase of electronic resources.

Placing paperbacks in a separate category will also show their reduced price. However, if paperbacks are not shelf-ready, and you have to catalog each separately, you will not be able to show your time as part of the cost. It is always difficult to justify the cost of your time.

On the other hand, differentiating between materials used for research placed in a reference section and materials used for research placed in a regular collection may be a very fine line. It may be considered that the more expensive materials balanced with the less expensive materials will balance each other out. Regardless of your decision, make sure that you still justify it and make the definitions clear to everyone who will be reading or listening to your budget presentation.

The average price for a library book is reported in a variety of places. The *Bowker Annual* is one authority, along with the *School Library Journal*. You may want to show a comparison of that figure with your own average cost. As noted previously, these figures may seem high, and invariably, someone reading your budget presentation will ask about the integrity of the calculation. The books that most people in the general public buy are paperbacks at the local bookstore or gift books during the holidays. Your cost will seem much more, and your audience will ask about discounts and other normal bulk buying practices. You will need to be able to discuss binding issues, costs associated with shelf-ready books, and MARC cataloging records.

This is where your data will be so much more valuable than using national data. If you know how much was spent in previous years, and how many books were purchased, you can do the math. In most instances where this has been done, school library media specialists have found that the national figures are very close. However, the fact that you have done the calculations based on local school data gives a preference for your data.

Divide the total number of books purchased by the amount spent on the purchase. Remember to include tax, shipping, and any pre-paid processing as well. Although some may argue that purchase processing should be included in other categories, the value of the time you will save is directly related to academic achievement. The question is how you as a certified and licensed teacher should spend your time. Should you spend your time in program administration doing a task that would cost a few extra dollars, or instructionally, which is important for student success and cannot be purchased so readily? No student ever thanked a librarian for the invaluable help provided by the expert cataloging.

In most cases, you will have two columns for the amount of money requested on books. The first is to bring the collection up to adequate levels, while the second is the amount requested to maintain the collection. This speaks again to the question of funding adequacy. We need to do much work as a field to decide the specifications for the second part of this equation.

Audiovisuals

The definition of audiovisuals is important to clarify for the budget audience. Print and non-print seem to have been the standard for some time, and most people were in school at the time of integrating films, video, and filmstrips. However, the inclusion of electronic materials in most library collections has added a third category. Materials such as videodiscs cross the line between traditional audiovisual and electronic materials. There is little help for clarification in standards and guidelines. Develop a definition that you are comfortable with and then go further to clarify with examples.

The average cost for audiovisual materials is very difficult to ascertain. Materials have dropped in price over the last few years. Formats have been invented, have risen in popularity, and have dropped almost entirely from use over the last several decades. At one time, 16mm films were several hundred dollars each, and libraries had film libraries at the building and district level, along with the equipment needed to show these films. Now, not only has the format disappeared from most collections, but in the transfer to video, the price dropped to below $50 per video. Filmstrips, film loops, and other similar audiovisual materials have disappeared from most school libraries. For this reason, it is usually not helpful to look at spending for audiovisual materials beyond the last two or three years.

By far the best way to ascertain the plan for videos is to look at teacher needs and requests over the last several years. Carefully-recorded teacher requests can document the unmet needs. While a small amount will be necessary to replace dated information, the need to replace dated formats is probably more crucial. New money will need to be budgeted for current and future teacher needs. Figure 6.3 shows one way that this information can be compiled.

Figure 6.3: Expenditures for Audiovisual Materials

Formats	Size of Existing Collection	Cost per Item Over Last Two Years	Cost of Replacement by Other Formats
16mm Films			
Filmstrips			
Audiorecordings			
Videodiscs			
Videos			
Non-Reference CD-ROM			
Other Sources			

Figure 6.3 will need to be adapted to meet the needs of your individual collection. Materials that are no longer usable but do not need to be replaced should be discarded at this time. Surveys of teachers are somewhat helpful to ascertain teacher needs, however, the best documentation comes from a careful, systematic review of each teaching unit upon completion. Interview teachers and ask them about the degree to which the collection met their teaching needs. This method gives needed context to the request, since it will not merely be thousands of dollars of audiovisuals to support the science curriculum but can be explained by examples (i.e., the ninth grade needs visual examples of cells or dissections). This creates an immediate response from parents in the audience, since they can connect with that unit with their children.

This is not the only way to establish a rationale for a budget figure. However, for this category especially, the procedure by which you arrived at the requested figure is very important. There are other alternative procedures you can adapt and implement, but you will have to be explicit about your decision processes.

Other Resources

The "other resources" category should be reserved for types of materials on which you spend so little that it is not worth a full budget discussion. You may decide to create categories for magazines, electronic resources, access or license agreements, or other types of materials and resources.

It may be true that the purchase of electronic resources has over time made it possible to reduce the number of magazine subscriptions. However, be sure to take into account the importance of magazines for leisure reading. Rather than reducing the amount spent for magazines, it may be an opportunity to increase the diversity of magazine subscriptions available to students. For non-readers intimidated at the prospect of reading an entire book, a magazine targeted to a specific hobby or an interest can make the difference between reading and not reading.

Repeat the process for other categories listed in Figure 5.5 and transfer the data to the charts in this chapter. Remember to make notes that justify purchases. Does your budget audience understand the types and purposes of magazines in the school library? What about supplies? The operation of the library program depends on smoothly functioning processes. These require supplies that are, for the most part, unfamiliar to those not intimately involved with libraries. The general public may not be aware of the variety of bar code labels, wands, or other specific supplies. Wherever possible, tie the supply budget to the instructional process. Consider the impact that posters and signs have on circulation. The speed by which books are processed and available for students depends on the supplies purchased for the program.

Establishing the Bottom Line

Stephen Covey, in his book *The 7 Habits of Highly Effective People* (1990), reviews the elements of win-win philosophy. He notes that there are three elements of win-win philosophy: Integrity—or knowing your own value; Maturity—the balance between courage and consideration; and Abundance Mentality—the sense that there is plenty out there for everyone (Covey, 1990, p. 217-220).

School library media specialists are not very good at demonstrating the character trait of an abundance mentality. Knowing in the past that there has been little money available for school library media programs, it is difficult to adopt the sharing mentality of win-win. We have to accept the fact that many of the reasons behind the lack of funding for school library media programs can be boiled down to this: we have not asked, and when we did, we did not justify our request.

This win-win philosophy will guide the remainder of the budget process. At the end, we will have to internalize that the value of the library program is worth a budget increase, and that if the library program wins, then everybody wins.

Follow the directions to fill in the spreadsheet in Figure 6.4. Remember, at the beginning of the chapter, it was stated that the process would be fuzzy. Use this worksheet as a guide.

Figure 6.4: Alternative Spreadsheet Example

	Average Price x Item	Required To Meet Standard	Total Budget Needed	Year One	Year Two	Year Three
Books						
Audiovisuals						
Facilities						
Equipment						
Staff						
Electronic Resources						
Other Types of Access						

In the first column, put the number you found by investigating your average price per item. Then, in the second column, refer back to the Chapter 5 to get the amount needed to bring the collection up the standard. Multiply to find the next number. Divide that column by three, and place that number in the three columns for year one, year two, and year three. To make things simpler, we will assume that the cost of living will remain roughly the same for all three years.

As you finish this spreadsheet, the temptation here will be to lower that figure, based on your knowledge of how little you have received in the past (they'll never give me that much) or on the financial status of the school district in the latest budget crisis (they don't have the money). Remember the Stephen Covey elements of the win-win philosophy. If you do not think your value equals that amount of money, then no one else will. What is the value of the library media program to the students? What impact will a strong collection have on reading test scores? What is the quality of the library media program that your students and faculty deserve? How much is your district willing to spend on proven processes that will improve student achievement and increase test scores? These are the questions that should guide you through this process.

Your role is to develop a budget request based on your own action research and the published research in the field. It is not your role to refuse to accept the needs of the students translated into the library media budget. There will be plenty of people who will take that role in your budget audience. Someone has to believe that the library program is worth the money you have determined it needs through your research. If you are not that person, then who will be?

The aforementioned process addresses one element of the library program budget, bringing the collection to standard. However, maintenance of the strong collection is also important. In the next section, a procedure is outlined to develop a maintenance budget for the school library media program.

Developing the Maintenance Budget

Remember the promise of the 1960 standards, which called for one new book per student per year. That figure is still valid. Remember, however, that some of the money that was spent on new books in the 1960s is now spent on electronic reference tools, such as encyclopedias and indexes. Place the amount spent on references in Figure 6.5. Then, look at your own collection and figure out what you would have spent maintaining the reference collection; remove that figure and place it in the electronic resources section. We know from the research listed in Chapter 2 that the numbers of books added to collection may have been more a function of budget than the addition of electronic resources. However, you can add to that data by assessing your own needs.

Are you buying fewer books and more electronic resources? Is that based on need or is it because of budget constraints? Figure 6.5 can help you with the thought process in order to develop a maintenance budget.

In the first column, put the number previously calculated as the average price per item. In the next column, put what you have determined to be the standard. The third column may evolve over time. Looking back over the last several years, knowing what has happened with loss rates, loss of currency, and new requirements for technology resources, try to place numbers in the third column that make sense to you.

Figure 6.5: Preparing the Maintenance Budget

	Average Price x Item	Standard	Total Maintenance Budget
Books			
Audiovisuals			
Facilities			
Equipment			
Staff			
Electronic Resources			
Other Types of Access			
Other Materials			

Don't forget the standard of one new book per student per year as a good place to start. For the other areas in the collection, you should survey the teachers and the students to determine how well the collection is meeting their needs. Not every collection is perfect, and there will always be unmet needs. However, there should not be gaping holes in the collection.

The *School Library Journal* surveys by Marilyn Miller and Marilyn Shontz are good sources for reviewing the average size of collections. These surveys, over time, have given an indication of the number of periodicals in a collection or the amount of audiovisual materials, along with needed context, that can provide good justification for the budget presentation.

Summary

Previously, we discussed the concept of funding adequacy, which can be defined as the amount of money required to make one student an effective user of ideas and information (AASL/AECT, 1998). As a profession, we need to do much more work with analyses of collections to determine which factors can be implemented in a formula to discover the funding adequacy formula for school library media programs. We are far away from that point.

However, for the collection in your school, you can now say with some authority what the collection needs are in your school and for your students. In Part 3, we will begin to implement the budget strategy.

At this point, you should know how much money you will need over the next several years in two categories: to bring the collection to standard and to maintain the collection. These numbers should not be discussed without context. In Part 3, we will prepare the budget presentation.

Revisit your mission and beliefs. It's normal to want to get right into the budget development process, to analyze the collection, and to create the charts and graphs of data that you will need. However, the plan will fall apart unless based on a strong mission and vision. Revisit Chapter 1, on the mission and beliefs, and also Chapter 4, on advocacy. Are you ready to begin this process?

Do you have a buddy? At times during this process, it is helpful to have a partner to share findings with and to double check results. See if someone else in the district can do this process with you, or perhaps find a library school student to work with you. The more results that are being talked about in the school district, the more likely this plan will be seen as an inevitable change.

What Would Savvy School Library Media Specialists Do?

Savvy school library media specialists know that they did not decide how much things cost. They understand they had nothing to do with the average price that was paid for a book. The fact that computers are expensive is not their fault.

Savvy school library media specialists don't apologize for wanting the best education possible for students and staff. They know their role as the information resource expert in the school, and they make a professional presentation based on the latest research in the field and their own action research.

Savvy school library media specialists believe that libraries are valuable. They request the amount needed for a library program that will benefit students and teachers. They can show directly how the program supports teachers and students.

Part 3

Putting the Plan Together

"How long 'till we get there?" That familiar backseat lament may sound tempting at this point. The long hours of research into past budget history, the hours spent on advocacy, and the organization of dry facts and figures into a spellbinding library story may seem to have taken years instead of hours. However, remember that the question above has a seldom-asked companion: "How far have we come?" If you shared your story as it developed and turned each statistics into an "AHA!" sound bite to be used in advocacy, chances are that you have already seen some budget increases.

Each turn in the road, however, only opens new horizons to be set as new goals. This chapter will help you to implement your budget plan to continually evolve as current goals are achieved and new goals discovered. "How long 'till we get there?" In this section, we will learn that the journey is the goal. Think about a sign in Bridgeville, Delaware: "If you lived here, you would be home by now." Living in the budget cycle not only means a constant striving but also a constant celebration as more and more pieces of the program fall into place to make your library program the best place it can be for students and teachers; the place where student achievement is visible not only on test scores but in the eagerness to learn.

Chapter 7

The Budget Presentation

By this time, you have spent hours gathering data, surveying teachers and students, and analyzing the collection. It must now seem anticlimactic that writing the actual budget presentation is only one chapter. Years of work, hours of data-gathering, late nights, early mornings, staring at columns of figures on a computer screen, and it comes down to a 20-minute budget presentation. The formal budget presentation should truly be the tip of the iceberg when it comes to the budget development process. In this chapter, we will review the writing and implementation of the formal budget plan.

In fighting for school district budget dollars, there sometimes seems to be an assumed antagonism between academics and athletics. The cost of athletic materials, sometimes perceived to be budgeted at the expense of library materials, makes these natural competitors. "We do without books, but the basketball team gets new uniforms." That may well be true. However, focusing on what other programs may have and what the library program does not have may seem petty to others. Remember the abundance mentality of Stephen Covey. There is plenty out there for everyone.

That said, in order to discover successful budget strategies, there is much to be learned from listening to school board debates about athletic expenditures. The cost of one football helmet, for instance, is close to $200. Each year, as the athletic budget is presented, the number and the costs of football helmets and other athletic equipment are presented. Although the school board may question the number of football helmets needed and whether there is a less expensive source available without sacrificing quality, the issue of whether or not to buy football helmets is never discussed. The expert, the district athletic director, may be quizzed on matters of cost and quality. When asked if he really needs all these helmets this year, his answer can be a terse, "Yes, unless you want me to have more kids cut from the team." This answer will be accepted, and most likely, his budget will be passed.

The most important question in the athletic budget discussion is never asked, and even to ask it would be seen as silly by all involved. That important question is, "Why do we need football helmets?" The answer has nothing to do with the relative importance of helmets over books. It has nothing to do with whether or not "they" like football better than "they" like libraries. The obvious answer to the question of why football helmets are needed is simply, "You can't play football without them."

Understanding the significance of that unasked question is crucial to developing a school library media budget implementation strategy. At a time when accountability is on the table facing every subject area, whether or not to play football is never discussed. The importance to students, to parents, to alumni, to the tradition and heritage of the school and, as a part of the success of the district is assumed. Districts may question the existence of the gifted program, the remedial education program, the driver's education program, and yes, even the library program. However, cutting a major sport from the athletic agenda, even if it is one that affects relatively few students, is never discussed.

Of course the school will have a football team, the absence of one is unthinkable. The library program needs to share that mentality.

"Of course we need these materials. You can't have a library program without them."

"Cut the leisure reading budget in half? Then there will be some students who may not read."

One of my favorite roadside signs is on Route 13, just outside of Bridgeville, Delaware: "If you lived here, you would be home by now." This is an important guidepost for this chapter. At this stage in the library budget cycle, we have to live in the library media program as if we were assuming our rightful place as the instructional leader, not as extra support or as enrichment. Research has shown that the core of an excellent instructional program is a strong library media program. We have to believe in the value of our own worth before we can expect others to believe it. One of the important ways that we can do this is to think of the instructional materials in the library media budget as not just for the library program. Everything in the library budget is of direct benefit to some curriculum area, some students or teachers, or another aspect of the instructional life of the school.

Writing the Budget Presentation

Upon reaching this point, you are beginning to make sense of the data. You should have a sense of the amount of money that is needed for maintenance of the collection or perhaps a larger figure that is needed for bring the collection up to standard. Those numbers, at this point, may seem extremely large. You may think your budget figures are pie in the sky and will never be funded. While that will be true for the first few years of implementation, the power of slow, steady pressure cannot be overstated or taken lightly.

Once you have the data thought out, then it is time to start writing the presentation plan. Boiling maple syrup is the best analogy to use with the budget presentation plan. Making a budget plan is like boiling maple syrup. It takes gallons of sap from the sugar maple tree to make a single pint of maple syrup. The sap is boiled for hours, condensing and evaporating the excess moisture in the sap down to the essence of maple syrup. A budget presentation is like that. The mounds of data that have been painstakingly collected must be grouped and presented as briefly as possible, probably totally less than 20 minutes. Data that took days to gather is summarized in either one line of a written text, a short paragraph, or as one small part of a budget chart or graph. The more concise your presentation is, the higher the chance that it will actually be read.

The word "presentation" is used deliberately. Generally a presentation is thought of as something that is presented. The visual image is one person standing in front of a group of people, showing charts and graphs. Remember that you are telling a story; one that may be told in a variety of different ways. At some point, you will do an actual presentation. Perhaps though, a written presentation of several pages complete with charts and graphs may be used. The value of an electronic presentation or a Web site is debatable. Certainly the links may be valuable, especially since you can then include a large amount of data for your readers to peruse as much as they care to. However, there is always some danger that without a great deal of text, some elements could be taken out of context. Some parts of the finalized budget plan may be used in reports, in advocacy activities, or in other ways to get your message across.

The following reviews the basic parts of a budget presentation. The format is not set in stone. You should adapt it to meet your personal presentation style and to match the style and format of other presentations given in the district. Remember, this is just a guide. Your audience should guide the development of the budget presentation.

Introduction to the Presentation

Introduce the budget plan in a very brief paragraph, usually one or two sentences. Talk briefly about how the budget was prepared and the research that went into the preparation of each section. The purpose of this introduction is to prepare the reader for the budget mindset. If the reader appreciates the mission and the beliefs of the library program and understands that the plan was built on sound research, then it is more likely that he or she will be open to what follows.

Start back with Chapter 1, when you began developing the mission and the vision of the school library media program. As you thought about your mission, you also thought of the mission of the school. Follow the format of Figure 7.1 to begin to justify the elements of the mission that the library program can begin to bring into reality. The following activity will help you to align your budget requests with the mission of the school. This will be the beginning of the budget implementation process.

Figure 7.1: Alignment of the School Library and School Missions

Elements of the School Library Media Mission	Elements of the School Mission	School Library Media Areas of Focus	Evidence
Ensure that students	Will be student-centered	Student-owned	Open access policy ensures that students can come to the library at any time
and staff		collaboration	Journal of instructional classes
are effective users	high achievers		Research base for school library program
of ideas	strong readers	reading encouragement	No limits on circulation, evidence of reading
and information	inquiring problem-solvers	information skills instructional program	Portfolio of student projects

Reading down the first column is the school library media mission from *Information Power*, "to ensure that students and staff are effective users of ideas and information" (AASL/AECT, 1998, p.7). Those elements are aligned with elements commonly found in schools and school districts. Your columns will look different, according to the specific mission of your school library program and your school. You may even choose to add columns, to include the school district mission, or to include the alignment of the *Information Power* mission with the school library media program mission, if it is different.

The last two columns give only one piece of evidence or one way that the school library media program supports the mission of the school. You may find that you have several ways that the library program can implement the parts of the school mission. Remember to just choose two or three. The analogy is feeding fish. A little fish food is necessary for survival, but it is easy to overfeed, with disastrous results. For the last column of the evidence, when detailing the evidence that shows how the library program is aligned with the school mission, be as specific as possible. Highlight instructional projects that went well and that came close to the ideal collaborative instructional class. Focus on what students learned, rather than materials or electronic tools used.

You will soon see that the library program in the school touches just about all parts of the mission of the school. If reading is stressed in the school, then obviously the library program is of prime importance. For a school focusing on creating informed citizens, the same is true for information literacy skills and awareness. In fact, it would be difficult to find a mission aimed at the children in the school that does not in some way touch the library program or in which the library program is not central to that mission.

Put this chart aside for the moment. For the next step, think of the values and the beliefs that you noted in Chapter 1. In the same way that you hope that your mission, your values, and your beliefs are explicit in the way you act, the way you teach, and even in the library policies and procedures, you can identify the values and the beliefs of others in the school.

When working on Figure 7.2, think of the phrases that you hear the school principal say every day. How does the library program relate to those favorite sayings? What is the culture of the school, as noted through the slogans, activities, and events? How does the school library media program relate to that culture? As you go through this exercise, you will see that not only does the library program underwrite the mission of the school, the library media program also helps to bring the values and beliefs of the staff into reality.

Figure 7.2: Values and Beliefs Worksheet

Administration and Selected Teachers	Teacher/ Administration Values and Beliefs	School Library Media Program Values and Beliefs	Evidence that the Library Program is Furthering Those Beliefs

Now we are ready to begin to write the first paragraph of the budget report. Remember the maple syrup analogy. In the same way, Figures 7.1 and 7.2 have to be synthesized in just one or two paragraphs. Start by highlighting important points, then start making phrases, then sentences. Remember that you will be making a budget presentation each year, so don't feel as though you have to catch everything and make every point possible. Something you don't have room to say this year can be put in next year's report or can be used in other presentations and advocacy activities.

Overall Justification

The list of questions that follow gives a framework to begin the work of preparing this part of the budgeting plan. The purpose of this exercise is to place you into the teachers' shoes. In order to gain classroom teacher support, the library media specialist must be well respected by the faculty and must be seen as a team player.

Considering the lack of understanding about school library media as a profession, this is not always easy. It doesn't help that while classroom teachers may have to fund classroom supplies with less than $100, the school library media specialist is seen as having thousands at his or her disposal. The library media program has to be seen as everyone's budget, rather than as a separate program under the control of one person.

Question 1. What's In It For Me?

Teachers may not be verbalizing this question, but they most likely will be thinking it. Some school library media specialists have found the concept of a curriculum map helpful. Based on the collection analysis, curriculum maps show how the library media center program and materials are of assistance to each curricular program. The *Information-Power School* (Hughess-Hassell & Wheelock, 2001) includes a step-by-step process and several examples to follow.

Note that reading is considered to be a part of each instructional program. The research on reading is clear. Students who read better are more successful in each curricular program (Krashen, 1993). Sometimes it's easy to link leisure reading only to language arts classes. However, it should be considered part of each subject area. Try to highlight this, and then share with school faculty specific items that will benefit them directly if your budget is passed.

Question 2. How Do You Know What I Need?

This question speaks to the data collection for the budget procedures. The collection development program, while not discussed in this book in detail, should have three basic components. The selections (1) should be based on authoritative reviews, (2) should be matched with the stated and explicit curriculum of the district, and (3) should be based on input from the school community as to their needs and interests. How the data is gathered from the school community and is presented back to the constituents for comment is important. The ways that input is gathered from students and teachers, through a suggestion box, through an element in the teacher newsletter, or through formal means, such as a survey, need to be gathered in a paragraph. An explanation on how input is entered into the budgeting and acquisitions process should be given.

Examples are very helpful. If you can point to examples of large expenditures, such as an electronic resource that has a specific use in the curriculum or a refurbishing of part of the collection, your program of tying selection to the needs of students and staff will be accepted. This exercise also helps with advocacy for the school library media program. Asking for input and feedback and giving a sense of understanding and empathy for the resource needs of the classroom teacher does much to encourage widespread acceptance of the library media program budget.

Question 3. What Will Happen If This Plan Becomes Reality?

The opposite question, of course, is what will happen if the plan is not funded? Classroom teachers need to be cognizant of the possibilities of the school library media budget and the possibilities that can be theirs if the plan becomes reality. This is more than just the "stuff" in the budget that can be used by specific teachers. This question is aimed at the instructional impact of the school library media budget. How will teachers teach differently? How will students learn differently?

More important than your articulation of these points is the extent to which others can articulate them for you. Are the other faculty members in the school avid supporters of the school library media budget? Do they see it as crucial to their success? The key to achieving this is to share the information that you have learned about the collection and to then share your proposed resolutions for collection issues and problem areas. As the library media program is described as the heart of the school, so should the library media program budget be described as the heart of the instructional budget.

This section needs to be summarized as briefly and concisely as possible. In just a few sentences, sum up the important points.

As an introduction to the next section, this overview should mention the intensive research process that uncovered basic problems with the collection, facilities, staff, or other areas. At this point, the budget categories listed in the next section, "Budget Body," should be mentioned. If in fact the budget is divided into two areas—bringing the collection to standard and continuously maintaining and improving the collection—then that should be stated, with a brief explanation of each.

Budget Body

The research underlying the budget plan can be outlined in two ways. Any research relating to the collection as a whole needs to be stated in the general overview section. The opening few sentences of that section can review the research process. However, research relating to specific parts of the collection will need to be in each of the specific sections that follow. The literature should be checked frequently for new studies or for action research that underscores your budget points. Pithy quotes are also helpful, either from the literature or from library users, including students or faculty.

Each section of the budget plan must be justified instructionally and must be inline with the terms of the mission of the school and the district. Specific initiatives should be addressed. The more important the initiative is to what gets funded, the more imperative it is that the initiative be addressed directly in the budget plan.

As you go through each section, make notes on the elements of your budget that you will want to include. After finishing each section, write a brief outline of what your budget presentation should include.

Books

Although most people would agree that books are important, their specific importance has to be stated. "Everyone" may know that reading is important, but we are learning more and more each year about the impact of strong reading skills on all aspects of academic achievement. Evidence that can be used includes circulation figures, which show how much the collection is used, the difference between the circulation of new books and that of older books, and other statistics.

Research on the importance of reading should be included here as well. Student's browsing nonfiction topics of interest, the importance of parallel reading, and the importance of breadth and depth of a basic nonfiction print collection need to be stated. Although the maintenance of the collection in terms of standards should be mentioned, the instructional use of resources will send a more powerful message than merely noting the collection needs to meet standards.

The student research process and the use of print resources in that process are crucial to mention. It is ironic that at the same time that the Internet is being hailed as containing all the answers for all student research, it is also being restricted by the use of filters. The value of print resources in student research needs to be articulated clearly. It might be helpful to mention some specific reference sources that are not available in electronic formats.

Describing resources gets rather boring extremely fast. It is always better to mention resources in the context of their use. Get in the habit of reading the "Works Cited" sections of student research projects. Ask for permission to copy those sections that illustrate the wide variety of resources available. We can talk about the value of print sources forever. However, noting that "these students received A's" and then showing the types and varieties of sources that they used will have tremendous impact among parents.

Of course, this speaks to the need to structure research assignments to give students experience in using a wide variety of resources. Collaborative instructional research projects can produce some impressive "Works Cited" pages that will demonstrate the power of the collaborative effort of the school library media specialist and the classroom teacher.

Magazines

As with books, there are quantitative standards to set the suggested numbers of magazines for a library media center. Remember that the audience will be most likely familiar with the type of magazines that they receive at home. Your audience may overlook the use of magazines for research projects and for reading encouragement. You should note their use in parallel reading assignments, for current events, and also for use in student research. If the electronic resources you are purchasing have allowed you to lower the number of total magazines purchased by the library program, it is important to mention that, not to show that sometimes budgeted amounts can go down, but also to justify an increase in the number of magazines, if possible.

The importance in leisure reading as a lifelong activity must be stressed as an activity that can be a strength of the library media program. Many times, reading is defined only as reading fiction, book-length novels. Developing the habit of reading a favorite magazine can be started at an early age. If we encourage students to read the weekly *Sports Illustrated, People, Time, Newsweek,* or any of the popular magazines, we may achieve more of our reading goals. For students who may never read a full-length novel completely, or at least willingly, we can offer in the school library media center materials in magazine format to meet their interests. Reading *NASCAR Today, WWF News,* or another magazine targeted to student interest may be the only way to create lifelong readers with some students.

Audiovisual Materials

Sometimes television and other audiovisual materials are automatically cast as instructional villains, as in the past, tired teachers may have reserved Friday afternoon to pull the shades, show endless videos, and lull the children into passive submission. The instructional use of audiovisual materials as just another type of informational resource should be reviewed.

Knowing that some in the audience may view audiovisual materials in a negative light, you should highlight some instances in which the use of video was able to demonstrate or to illustrate something for the students in a way that still pictures or print descriptions could not do.

A summary of the types of audiovisual materials included in the budget is crucial. You may need to review the formats of audiovisual materials. Charts are helpful to show the use of the collection by curriculum content area as compared with the percentage of the collection available.

It is a good idea when describing proposed additions to the collections to review how they will be used, with as many specifics as possible. This is a great way to elicit help from the rest of the faculty in gathering support for the budget presentation. Mentioning the use a science teacher will make of a videodisc may garner automatic nods from any other science faculty in the audience. The addition of a videotape series reviewing the battles of the Civil War will get smiles and thoughtful responses from parents in the audience whose children may have just taken or who are about to take U.S. History, especially if you have a tentative plan with the classroom teacher on how this resource will be used with students and teachers.

Remember, however, that your time is limited. Give several brief examples and use different classroom teachers and grade levels of students. The impression that you want to give is that this is not the library budget. This is the school instructional resource budget. Giving specific examples of use is easy to do with audiovisuals because they are used more by teachers and are used more directly in the classroom to teach instructional content.

Even though audiovisual materials have been around for some time, this may be one of the more difficult sections to write. The definition of what constitutes an audiovisual material and the instructional value of audiovisuals to the academic life of the school may vary widely, according to your listeners' past experiences and their informed or uninformed opinions. It will be up to you, in just a few sentences, to correct their misinterpretations, to give your definition, and to present a valid instructional foundation for the use of these resources. The first step, of course, is to make sure that you have a strong definition of what you consider audiovisual resources to be as opposed to electronic or other types of materials. Books with accompanying tapes, for example, could be either considered part of the print collection or an audiovisual resource. There is very little right or wrong here. The only caution is that you need to make it clear to your audience.

Electronic Resources and Computers

Electronic resources generally fall into two categories: electronic reference tools and technology for technical services and program administration. This is another category with a fuzzy definition. On one hand, including all types of electronic resources, all licensing agreements, and all new types of electronic resource equipment, such as digital cameras, scanners, or other electronic resources, may present a total picture for the audience.

On the other hand, a separate category for equipment, even though it can be thought of as similar to other electronic resources, may be necessary according to the school district budget procedures manual. Licensing agreements may be a complicated enough subset to warrant a completely different category.

Usually, it is a good idea to separate licensing agreements for technical services and products, such as the automated catalog, from electronic resources. Technical services are a program administration function and will muddy the waters of your argument for electronic reference tools.

How students and teachers use electronic reference sources will need to be reviewed, along with any use statistics. Remember that cost efficiency is always the cost of the resources divided by the number of uses. For the higher cost items, a high level of use should be expected, unless the material is targeted for a specific subject or for a specific group of users. It is more effective to point out that an electronic magazine index cost $0.03 per use than to note that it was several thousand dollars. Cost per student is another way to present information in order to demonstrate the value of an electronic resource to the instructional program in the school.

Some hardware and access issues should be considered here. Limiting printing means lowering the cost efficiency of the product, since students who are forced to copy notes from the screen are preventing other users from accessing the resource.

Equipment needs, if combined in this category, should be tied directly back to instructional use. The amount of time students are accessing the computers, the average wait time (if there is one), and the types of uses that the machines are receiving are all important points.

For people in the audience who have a home computer, their only electronic access may be Internet web pages. The concept of proprietary databases, of controlled vocabulary, and of controlled access may be a completely foreign concept. It is easier to demonstrate the difference by giving instructional examples than it is to lecture with educational or library jargon.

Be simple, try to use examples from your personal experiences or your students and be concise. There are still people who do not believe that computers have a place in school; they may think that using a magazine index may be "cheating." You will have a few seconds in a presentation, or a few lines on a written page, to change that mindset.

Supplies

This category is perhaps the most difficult to justify instructionally. Even though it is perfectly obvious that supplies are needed to run a library, it is still very important to tie these supplies to instruction, even indirectly. The use of signs and the purchase of incentives, even things such as bar code labels, are essential. Supplies make use of the library materials possible, which is essential for cost efficiency. Without supplies, the materials cannot get to the students. Make a list of the supplies that you order and attempt to determine the instructional value for each. As a last step, summarize that list in one paragraph, giving specific examples of perhaps one or two items.

Continue this process with all other categories. Note that we have not used a separate category for equipment. Although that is normal practice, it is the category that is always least likely to be funded. Try including audiovisual equipment with audiovisual materials and computer equipment with electronic resources. This makes the expenditure a lot easier to justify and much harder to cut.

Budget Summary

You may feel that you have information left unspoken, perhaps something that may not have exactly fit in the program. Try giving a "Frequently Asked Questions" handout, similar to the one shown in Figure 7.3. This accomplishes two goals. First, it allows you the opportunity to give out information that would not have been a good "fit" in your budget presentation. Second, it allows you to take control of possible questions that may be difficult to answer. You control how the question is worded, so that you can give the answer likely to be the most effective. You can also speak from a national perspective.

Figure 7.3: Frequently Asked Questions about Library Budgets

Q. **We seem to be buying stuff for school libraries, classroom libraries, and public libraries. Isn't that a duplication?**

A. The public library is an important community resource and works with the school library to provide the best services. Remember, though, that the public library has a different mission. The school library has a curriculum that is integrated with all other subjects in the school. The school library is also open and available to students and the teachers throughout the school day. The public library and limited classroom libraries are an important help, but the school library is the main supporter of the learning process.

Q. **With electronic resources, do you still need books?**

A. In this budget, I have shown areas in which the purchase of electronic resources has replaced the purchase of print materials. Replacing magazines with full-text magazine databases will replace some magazines. Remember, however, that reading is still one of the most important skills that students will learn. Good readers want to read, and we have to have materials in the school library that encourage children to want to practice their reading skills.

Other Questions

Q. **The Internet is free, isn't it? Why do you need all of these other computer resources?**

Q. **How does this budget compare with other area schools?**

Remember also that you may get some difficult questions, especially if you have had a challenge or have weeded heavily. You need to be prepared to answer those, but always bring the answer back to the budget.

At the end of the budget presentation, you should include a sentence or two to sum up the presentation. Consider carefully the one thought you would like to leave your audience with. Try a quote from a student, a story about an instructional project, or a quote from the literature.

In Figure 7.4, the details of Chapter 7 are presented in outline form. Your actual presentation could be very different, since it should be based on the research that you have done in your library media center program.

Figure 7.4: Budget Presentation Plan Overview

The Budget Presentation Plan

	Length	Contains
Introduction	1-2 paragraphs	■ Review of the overall process ■ Alignment of Missions ■ Link to Values and Beliefs
Overall Justification	1 paragraph	■ Reasons for support of the budget ■ Examples of benefits to the school community
Budget Body ■ Books ■ Magazines ■ Audiovisual Materials ■ Electronic Resources	1 paragraph each	Instructional justifications ■ Reading and print research sources ■ Use in lifelong reading ■ Use in student research ■ Instructional use ■ Importance of media literacy skills ■ Research use as opposed to home skills
Summary	1-2 sentences	Quote or other memorable statement

Figure 7.4 is only one possibility for a budget presentation. Based on your data, you should choose the budget defense that would present the information in the best format. It is also wise to follow any district format that is spelled out in the budget policy manual.

The budget plan should only be several pages in length. Any longer than that, and you may find that you have lost your audience, which is wandering around in the forest. Your job here is to identify trees. Be concise and to the point with each area in the budget defense.

Try these tricks to lower the length.

■ Read each paragraph and then summarize to yourself what you just said. Review your summarization to see if you can state the same information more concisely.
■ Ask someone else to review and to cut where necessary.
■ Use charts and graphs to summarize information.
■ Focus on one or two instructional justifications instead of trying to list every single reason why things should be purchased.

- For categories for which you are listing instructional areas that will be positively impacted, try just listing one or two areas as examples.

Budget Implementation

By this point in the chapter, you should have a well-written budget plan. It is now time to begin the implementation of the budget plan. You may feel that you are not ready at this point. You may feel that you need to do more work on your plan before you present it. You may feel that the timing is not right or that the district is not in the mood to hear a request for money. However, most likely, no matter how much work you put into your budget plan, that feeling will never go away. You are as ready now as you can be at this time. Rather than waste another minute in an unfunded state, it is now time to begin the implementation.

Before Beginning

The time to begin the implementation of the budget plan is when you first pick up this book. Although there are negative connotations of living in a sound-bite world, in this case, it can be used to your advantage. As you work through the processes in this book, you will end up with far more data than you can actually use in the budget presentation. It will be better to use pieces of your findings in short statements or in paragraphs that are worked into other reports than to keep them secret until the presentation.

As stated earlier, by the time of the budget presentation, your audience should already be familiar with what you are going to say in your budget presentation. As you discover more and more information about the history of expenditures or from the analysis of the collection, share that information.

Below are listed some places where you can use the data.

- **Monthly Reports to the Principal**—The monthly report to the principal is an excellent way to concisely present information regarding progress in school library media program goals. Never more than one page, it can contain information about circulation, highlights of collaboration, library program news, and of course, information about your budget progress.
- **Parent Newsletters**—Most school administrators are reluctant to put any negative news in parent or community newsletters. However, interesting, did-you-know tidbits about national data, the average price of a library book, and other data will be acceptable. You do not have to mention the connection with the library budget. Supporters and non-supporters alike will eventually get tired of being constantly pounded by the library budget hammer. You are planting seeds, not giant redwoods. Try to make sure that the principal has interesting tidbits that parents would find useful or interesting and that can be put in newsletters as fillers. You can also write a longer article about library goals or other issues. Look back at the overview of the budget presentation. Each one of the points that you summed up in one sentence can be easily reviewed in greater depth in an article.

- **Faculty Newsletters or Library Web site**—Again, you do not want to paint a negative picture of the school in any public forum. However, simple statements of fact based on faculty surveys, on comparisons with national data, and on other research pieces are fine to include, especially if you do not expound on the negative elements. Issues of *Book Report* magazine or *School Library Media Activities Monthly* always carry interesting articles on collaborative project. Your faculty may find it interesting to know what other people are doing, and they may come to you to ask for the same resource so that they can do that project with you.

When conducting budget research, as many people as possible should be aware of what you are doing and what you have found at each stage of the process. With each piece of data, consider who is affected by it? Who should be made aware of the consequences of the uncorrected situation?

Making the Presentation

It is part of the job responsibility of each school library media specialist to annually prepare a budget presentation. Very few school library media specialists will be expected to actually present it to an audience. However, whether asked or not, the written report should be given annually to the building principal, chair of the site-based management team, or the district supervisor. In rare cases, the building principal may actively discourage the budget request. In that case, make sure that the building principal gets the information through monthly reports or e-mail updates, but don't refer to them as budget requests. A series of "For Your Information" memos can be used to submit all the information contained in the budget presentation.

If permitted to do the presentation, especially if it is for the site-based management team, make sure that you know your audience. Place yourself in the position of each member of the team. Make sure that each point will resonate with a member of the team.

Include visuals that reflect the professional nature of the presentation. Use of color is key for clarity of points. Use the highest level of technology available for the presentation, but be careful. There may be both technophiles and technophobes in the budget audience. Their perceptions of your data will vary depending on their feelings toward how you use technology.

Give handouts of the slides used in the presentations. A nice touch is to give a written copy of the presentation and a duplicate of the presentation slides in handout form. This give the budget text that the team can peruse later, and yet they will still be able to follow your presentation.

Allow time for questions. For most presentations, about 20 minutes is the optimum time to present data, with at least 10 minutes for questions. It is up to you whether you prefer questions at the end, or whether you would like questions as you go along. A good strategy is to let that unfold naturally.

To encourage questions, smile and look directly at individuals across the table.

Allow at least one minute (which will seem like forever) for someone to formulate a question. Some presenters use the strategy of developing their own questions and giving them to friends to ask to spark questions. Since it is impossible to judge the presentation flow or the atmosphere beforehand, planned questions can seem rather stilted and unnatural. It may be better to start by saying, "I was hoping someone would ask this question ... so I will ask it myself ..."

After the Presentation

At the conclusion of the presentation, thank the team for allowing you to present. If possible, stay in the room until there is a natural break. This will give some time for team members to approach you individually with questions that did not occur to them or that they did not want to ask in public.

In some districts, writing or e-mailing thank-you's to the budget team may be appropriate. If members of the team expressed an interest in follow-up data, try to get that to them within one week of the presentation.

Presentations Without Presenting

If there is no site-based management team or district-based budgeting team, there is usually no audience for a presentation. You may simply give the principal a copy of the written text and should be available for questions. However, there are other strategies to fund budget needs using a variety of district budget streams.

Do you know who has budget authority in the district? A review of the budget manual should tell you which administrators have budget authority. Try submitting pieces of the science materials and the equipment budget to the science supervisor and other pieces to other appropriate administrators. The gifted program usually stresses reading and inquiry learning and may use the library intensely. You may want to approach the gifted teacher with possible resources that you simply do not have the money to buy. The same is true of the special education teacher. In times of limited budgets, sometimes those teachers funded by federal programs will have money for materials.

Take advantage of special initiatives. The announcement that the superintendent is formulating a special committee on multicultural issues might be a good time for a list of parallel reading suggestions to be forwarded to the chair of the committee.

Other Tips

Work with other library media specialists in the district. Although each school is different, remember that the organizational structure narrows as it moves toward the superintendent. Are all the school library media specialists in the district using the same words to construct the budget message? Do you have the same goals? Visualize a group of building administrators at a district principal's meeting. The library program is mentioned, and one principal states what his or her library media specialist is stating that "libraries" want. Another principal looks puzzled and makes an opposite statement. A great opportunity is lost, and the unspoken message is "come back when you decide." If there is confusion on budget goals, chances are, nothing will be funded.

Consider the opposite. An issue is raised, and it becomes apparent that each library media specialist has informed the building principal of the library stance. An issue that may not have been considered library-related before now has an excellent chance of being funded.

Of course, it is much easier if there is district-level coordination, but even without a district library supervisor, groups of library media specialists can still meet for lunch, after breakfast, or on Friday night to celebrate the week. Do not be afraid to ask for time to meet. A principal is more likely than you think to agree for you to come in late one morning each month so that you can meet with your peers for breakfast. You really do not know until you ask.

Summary

The fear of being conspicuous keeps many school library media specialists from implementing their budget plans. Some may feel that it is not being a team player to ask for more than other people in the school have. A group of the teachers in the school may scoff and moan at the politics that are rife in school districts and may vow to not be a part of it. That makes it difficult to do what some would call "playing the game."

This is all true. There may be people in the district who think that your place is similar to the traditional advice given to the mother of the groom during wedding planning: keep your head down and your mouth shut, and wear beige. However, if you do not take an active role and do not have an active voice in the development of the library media budget, then who will do that for you? Who else is responsible for ensuring equal access to materials and resources for all students in the school? Who else has the mission that reaches out to encompass the entire school's instruction life?

Of course, you may encounter some resistance to being a strong advocate for the use of instructional resources in the school. There may be some faculty who will never understand how the library program can be an instrumental partner in the success of his or her teaching; and there will be some who see the library media program budget as competition for departmental or classroom funds.

But there is also pain in not having an adequate budget, in not being able to meet the needs of students and teachers, and in not being able to fulfill your mission. The choice is up to you.

For You To Do

Practice being concise. Remember the old TV game show *Name That Tune*. Write a paragraph of the budget presentation, and then remove half of the words. Try bullets, short captions, graphs, and other tips to shorten the number of pages.

Practice! Videotape yourself as you give the budget presentation to the site-based management team. Then videotape yourself giving the same talk to a group of administrators or to the school board. Do you talk the same way? Do you use the same words?

What Would Savvy School Library Media Specialists Do?

Savvy school library media specialists present a budget snippet with every memo and with most conversations. They include a graph of their latest findings, a "did you know" section in the newsletter, and regularly offer e-mail updates to their administrators. By the time the budget is presented, the content is well known.

Savvy school library media specialists know their audience. They know if stories and scenarios will be welcomed or resented. They know if some in the audience need facts and figures or want examples of implementation.

Savvy school library media specialists attend other budget presentations. This creates a "we're all in this together" mentality with other budget presenters. Watching and listening to other presentations also gives an indication of how your budget will be perceived, and it also helps to know what other people are buying.

Chapter 8

Other Issues of Budgeting

Many books on budgeting focus on alternative sources of funding, such as grant writing or fund raising (Morris, 2000; Hall-Ellis, 1999; Bauer, 1999). This book has focused thus far on the traditional budget structure and the process of the school district. It does this for a specific reason. It is the responsibility of the school district to fund the library program. Other types of funding sources, grant writing, book fairs and fund raisers, and lobbying for donations, are important, but they take time. Funding instruction is the responsibility of the school district. If we believe that the library program is truly at the heart of the instructional program, then abdication of that responsibility cannot be tolerated.

The Value of Time

Economists use a phrase to describe the choices that we make. "Opportunity cost" is the cost of choosing one activity over another. We would do well to work that phrase into monthly reports and budget presentations. Robert Frost's poem "The Road Less Traveled" is a wonderful poetic explanation of the dilemma of opportunity cost.

When we make a choice between two activities, each has some benefit to us.

When we choose one, we lose the benefit of the other. There is a profit from doing a book fair, however, the cost of the instructional time lost must be figured into the equation. The same is true of grant opportunities. The No Child Left Behind Act <http://www.nochildleftbehind.gov> is one example of a grant opportunity that should be pursued by all eligible districts. Although the possibility of funding is worth the time, the hours spent researching and filling out the grant application have to be counted as part of the cost.

While involved in meetings, counting change, and preparing grant applications, consider what are you not doing and what those missed instructional events mean to students. Book fairs or other fund raisers need to be balanced with the amount of time that it takes to host a successful fund-raising event. That time is lost from instructional use and must be accounted for.

This does not mean that these activities should not be pursued. However, the opportunity cost should be noted and should be presented as part of the report to administrators. This time does not necessarily need to be translated into dollars. It may be enough to state in a report to the administrators: "The book fair made $1,000. It took 15 hours of my time to prepare, to host the book fair, and to do the clerical work involved." Go into some detail in the report of what you weren't doing as a statement of fact or as a dilemma, not as a negative whine. Did you have to reschedule classes, turn away other instructional projects, or not gather books or materials for teachers? Brainstorm in the report what could be done to make the process more efficient.

The same is true of grant writing. As lawyers and accountants keep track of "billable hours" spent on projects, so should you. One of the major problems in the field is overcoming the image of school library media specialists in the back room reading magazines and clipping coupons while classroom teachers are teaching all day. Although the field is rife with rumors of this and other equally depressing images that are being reinforced every day by incompetent school library media specialists, we need to do more to show how our "back room" work is instructionally important.

Fund Raising

Book fairs are a common form of fund raising in school libraries. Book fairs fulfill an important instructional goal in that they show students, who may have never visited a bookstore, the allure of new books and of book ownership. Book ownership, according to Jim Trelease (1982), is one of the important three B's, the other two being bookshelves in the children's room, and reading in bed, that help to make children become avid readers.

Other popular forms of fund raising include special events or booths at field days, at sporting events, or at other activities. Including volunteers from the school community to help plan, staff, and manage the event can lessen the great amount of time spent in putting on a fund-raising event.

Fund raising is most successful when it is targeted to a specific need. Most people will support a fund-raising effort to "help the library." However, holding an event to bring the poetry section up to the standard needed for the language arts curriculum is a more targeted goal that could generate more results. Use the data gathered from budget research to plan and target fund-raising goals. The Media Advisory Committee or an organized parent volunteer group may have ideas of its own. Present to them the areas of greatest need not covered in the budget and see if the idea of fund raising springs up on its own accord.

Remember that you do not need to be in charge. If the Media Advisory Committee or a parent group decides that it wants to raise money to renovate the reference section, your role is to support that effort, not necessarily to coordinate, chair, or fulfill a leadership role. Your time can then be spent in instructional activities, rather than making phone calls and blowing up balloons.

Grants

The No Children Left Behind Act and the grant program associated with it may be beginning of a new era of competitive grant funding for school library resources. This is a far cry from the early days of Elementary and Secondary Education Act funding, when virtually all libraries received massive amounts of funding. The new wave of grant competitions requires data and research. The budget process outlined in this book can provide that research base for grant funding.

There are many books available on grant writing, and those school library media specialists interested in pursuing grants should make use of that expert help in writing. To make the best use of time, however, read carefully the eligibility requirements for the grant. Estimate the amount of time needed to apply for the grant and gain the support of the principal for the grant effort. Form a committee to review the grant application and to help with data gathering, with writing, and with editing the grant application. And finally, be sure to meet all deadlines.

There is a problem associated with grant funding, especially large grants. Although the possibility of thousands of dollars dropped from the sky by federal grants is enticing, remember the lessons taught by the massive federal funding in the 1960s and the early Seventies. Having thousands of dollars spent on school library collections and then not being able to replace and update those collections is how we got here in the first place.

Remember that a large amount of money spent at one time does not have the same effect as it would if spread out over time. With the rate at which books go out of print, a large one-time purchase of materials will fund only those resources currently available for sale. Books and other materials that were available last year, or that will be available next year, will not be purchased. Although large expenditures can help bring poor collections up to standard, maintenance funds will be needed to keep the collection at standard.

The action research that you are doing to support your budget request can be used very nicely in grant applications. Most grants require the use of data to show need. Your budget presentation work as outlined in this book already contains much of the data that you need. Grants can bring in funds for large-scale collection or for facility renovation that the school district budget may be more reluctant to support.

Gifts and Donations

Some school library media specialists are excellent at garnering donations and gifts for the library media program. Strategies include forming a "friends of the library" group, approaching the parent teacher association or student clubs, or even naming the school library media center after a potential benefactor.

One savvy school library media specialist, in a time of budget crisis, approached student clubs to replace magazine subscriptions that had been cut from the school library media program budget. The history club agreed to replace several history-oriented magazines, the science club agreed to do the same for science magazines, and so on throughout the school. Although as a long-term strategy this refutes the principle that the school district community has a responsibility to fund education for the students, it does make the student clubs feel more ownership for the library media center program. It is a short-term budget strategy in times of budget crisis, but in that context, it works well.

Community groups can also be approached for gifts and donations with permission of the principal. Again, it is much easier to persuade people to donate for a specific cause, rather than for a general or vague purpose. Buying something for a specific group of students, so that they can learn a specific topic better, has a good chance of being funded.

Other Department Budgets

The library media program is a reflection of the school curriculum. By browsing through the shelves and looking at the library collection, one should be able to gain a sense of the subjects taught in that school. The reverse is also true. As the library media program budget supports the subject curriculum by providing resources, so can the subject area budget provide resources for school library media materials and services.

When new curriculum is developed for the school, money should be included for new resources. The school library media specialist may need to present research showing the lack of key resources for the new curricula or may need to develop surveys to assess new technologies or electronic resources needed to teach the new curricula. In the beginning, this will be a great deal of work. However, as including money for school library resources becomes the norm rather than the exception, this process will become institutionalized. The library media specialist may be asked how much money should be included for resources, rather than the reverse.

Summary

Making use of alternative sources of funding is an important activity. It shows that the school library media specialist is doing everything possible to provide the most resources for students and staff. It can provide needed stop-gap funding, or it can fill in holes in the collection.

However, alternative funding will never replace a stable budget stream through the school district budget process. John Dewey set the standard over 100 years ago when he wrote "what the best and wisest parent wants for his own child, thus should the community want for all of its children" (Dewey, 1910; Dworkin, 1959, p. 34). The role of the school library media specialist in the process is to show cause—through research, data gathering, and steady pressure—why the community should want to provide equitable access to library resources and services for all its children.

Chapter 9

Furthering the Vision

Wow. All finished. You have the budget plan developed, presented, and it seemed to go well. Now you can put the plan aside and concentrate on other things.

Sorry, that's not how it goes. Change takes three to five years of effort before real progress to be made. At this same time, the annual budgeting cycle repeats itself, needs change, and school district finance opportunities will change as well. You had all the data you needed on your collection, and a major grant effort came through. Now everything is changed. Even while your plan was being developed, most likely there were changes in the school district that caused you to make changes in the budget plan. Perhaps the school picked up fifth graders at the middle school level or became an intermediate school of third through fifth grades rather than kindergarten through fifth grade.

Regardless, every time you think you are finished, it seems to start all over again. The good news is that the preliminary research on the historical picture of budgeting for your school library will not have to be redone. All that you will have to do is keep adding elements to clarify and to enhance that picture. However, the not-so-good news is that the work of budget implementation is never ending.

The budget wheel illustrates this. In its stationary form, the individual parts of the wheel are easy to see, and we are able to look at each part intensely and separately, as we have done in each chapter of this book. Once the wheel is in motion, however, it is no longer possible to see the individual sections. They whirl past faster and faster, until the budget cycle becomes a smooth blur.

Figure 9.1: The Budget Cycle

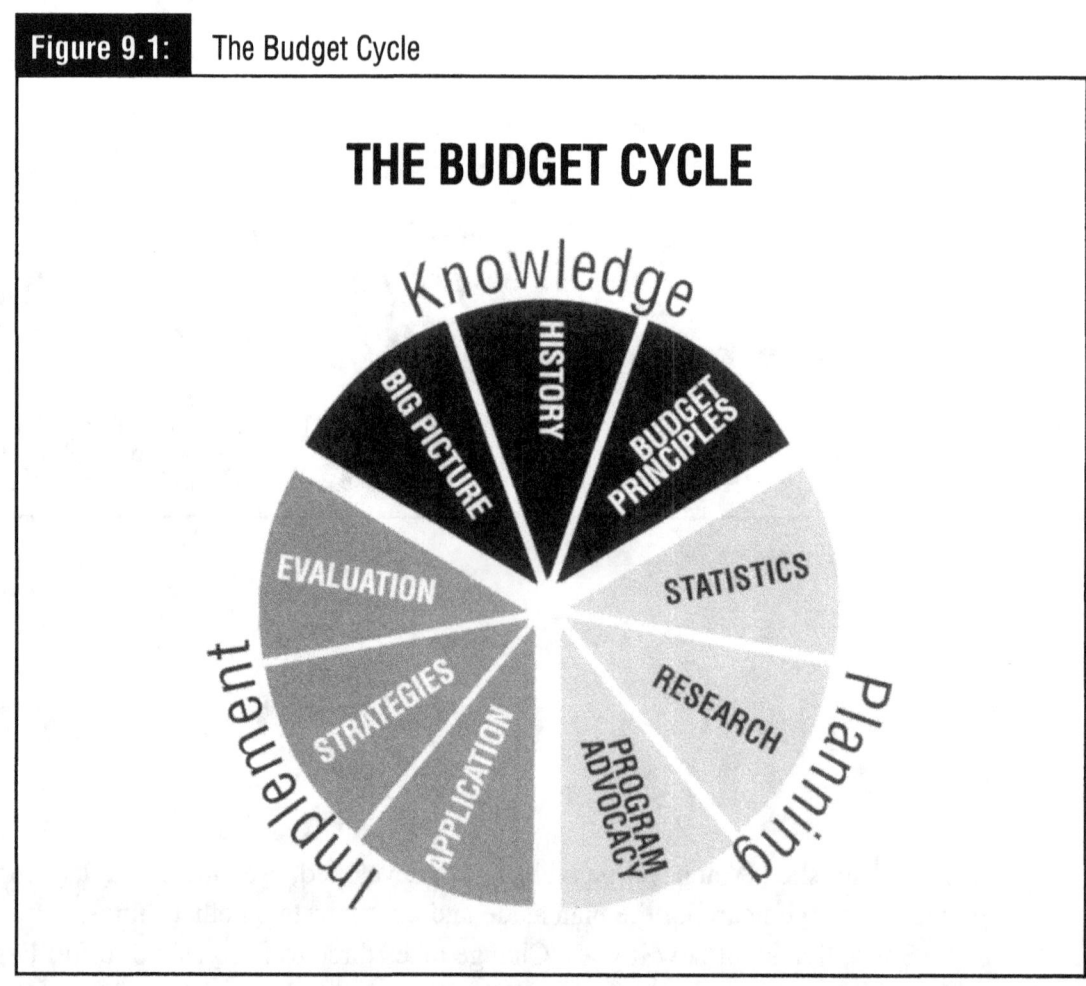

That is truly a representation of the budget cycle. The first time through, each stage was conducted separately. However, as the implementation progresses, new statistics will become available to use as comparable data. New research will be published that will further state your case. You will also find successes. Think of the budget process not as a road that can be traversed but as a front on a weather map, with lines that dip and swirl.

As the budget is implemented, your vision will be changed by new initiatives that are planned within the school and district and within the library program. Keep changing the written version of your vision to keep pace with the changes that you have. As each new area is funded, you should be able to see further what is now possible and should make the changes necessary to further the budget plan.

Samuel Gompers, in the early days of unionism, was once asked what does the

American worker want. His answer in one word, "More." Your answer will be the same, but the underlying reasons for that answer must be based on the greater good for the school community. If your budget is perceived as feathering the library cap, others will be reluctant to see your areas of influence grow. However, what if the library budget is perceived to be the one budget that benefits everyone in the building? If others perceive that through focusing on the instructional hub of the school, all roads benefit, then the question, "What does the library budget want?" can be answered in unison, "More." Students will always have more needs than we can answer.

It all comes back to what is best for students and what is best for teachers. Many have called the library media program the heart or hub of the school. However, that is still isolating. I prefer making the library program analogous to the climate control system. Students cannot learn and teachers cannot teach without heat in the winter or air conditioning in the summer. The library media program furthers the teaching and the learning of everyone in the school by providing resources and instruction to make learning happen in the best possible climate. Yes, students can still go to school in 95-degree heat, but they won't be learning much, and teachers will find that simply getting through the day, not instruction, will be the goal.

Strong library programs are more than resources, but it's difficult to have a strong library program without a strong budget. This book covered much more than just financial and accounting strategy. To have a strong budget presentation, one must have a strong instructional program, a strong reading encouragement program, and excellent relationships with teaching peers. This book has touched on collection development, on general management of the library program, and on advocacy, and just about all other areas of the school library media program in the school.

The budget wheel drives the school library media program. Without money, it is impossible to have the strongest possible individual pieces of the program. Strong elements of the program make the budget presentation stronger. Getting the data together, coordinating and aligning the elements of the program, and sharing what it all means to the instruction of students is crucial to both a strong program and a strong stable budget stream.

Does it work? Those people who have followed the processes in this book have seen their budgets increased and have been joined by their peers in the school in support of a strong, stable library program. You can too.

Remember the sign in Bridgeville, Delaware: "If you lived here, you would be home by now." The decision to live in the environment outlined in this book is yours.

Appendix A

Rocky Hill Middle School Budget Presentation

    AUDIENCE: Building principal
                          Site-based team
    FORMAT: Written document, no formal presentation
    SCHOOL: 500 students

To "educate responsible citizens and lifelong learners" is the mission of Rocky Hill Middle School. The library media program supports and furthers that mission "to ensure that students and staff are independent users of information and ideas." These are skills and attributes that our students will need in order to be responsible citizens and lifelong learners.

    The library media staff believes that our department encompasses the learning and teaching environment of the entire school. We believe that each child should love to read, should be an eager and inquiring researcher, and should look back on his or her middle school days as some of the best years of their education. To do that, we believe that we need a collection of resources, that are housed in the school, in the community and greater education community, and that are drawn from the best resources that exist in other formats, in order to meet curricular needs and student interests. Program facilities and technologies allow students and staff to use that collection most efficiently.

    To prepare this budget, the library staff engaged in an intensive action research project. We analyzed the library facility by comparing it with the state requirements. We analyzed past budgets and performed a collection analysis to determine the past history and current condition of the collection. We also used curriculum maps to match the in-house collection and resources outside the school to determine focused growth areas for the collection. And, most importantly, we surveyed students and staff, both formally and informally, to determine if the collection matched the interests of students. We then prioritized areas of the curriculum standards and teacher focus.

Books

Our collection analysis showed that only 10% of our collection was copyrighted after 1990. This means that 90% of our book collection was published before our students were born. Our curriculum map project, which was a collaborative instructional project with the English and Art departments, showed that we have several areas of the collection that are in the most need. Our collection still reflects the Soviet Union as one country, does not mention the Euro as a form of currency, and does not show the discoveries of the last decade in the astronomy or other sciences. We have had some success with increasing the size of the paperback collection to encourage student leisure reading. The test score increases with the sixth and seventh grades in this area are promising.

REQUESTED: $5,000 – general improvement of the collection
$500 – paperbacks to support leisure reading interests *
matched by the PTA
$1,500 – to address the most serious collection deficiencies

Magazines

The reading committee is very pleased with the success of our magazine initiative this year. Mrs. Jones and Mr. Evans have been very successful in their efforts to encourage more parents to donate old magazines they receive at home. The NASCAR and other sports magazines have been very well read. The reading committee has requested that the magazine budget be increased by 10 magazines, chosen as a result of the student survey. The committee feels this addition will encourage our efforts to increase reading as a voluntary leisure activity by students.

REQUESTED: $1,500

Audiovisual Materials

The media advisory committee has spent the last several months focusing on media literacy. The committee has formed an Audiovisuals Task Force of parents and faculty to discuss to what extent audiovisual materials can be used by students. Their report indicated that students can gain needed information by watching and taking notes from videos. The first media literacy classes have been integrated in several core areas and have been very successful. Teachers indicate that students who use audiovisuals in their research still use as much or more print materials. The Task Force has prepared a budget based on teacher requests for areas they feel are of the most need.

REQUESTED: $3,500

Electronic Resources

As noted in the PTA presentation about Internet research, electronic research databases are widely used by students. Our newest magazine index which contains the full-text of almost 1,000 magazines is widely used by students, and teachers have commented that the quality of the student research is improving steadily. The widespread use has brought that cost down to $0.03 per student use. As with most of these resources, license agreements on an annual basis allow us to have the most current resources and have also kept the cost down by staggering the implementation of new resources. The license agreement for the library automation system is also included.

REQUESTED: $3,500

Supplies

We have worked very hard to minimize the amount of supplies needed for the library program. We reuse and recycle copy paper into scratch pads for the computer. We use the e-mail system for student reminders and for teacher communication. Still, a library program runs on supplies to enhance instruction. It has been pointed out to library staff that new students have a difficult time finding the library. Therefore, the only new expense in this budget is signage to point to the library from various places in the school. We think this will help new students feel welcomed and will remind current students to visit the library.

Summary

It has been said, "It takes a village to raise a child." The library media program is the town center of that village. It is the hub, the marketplace, the park, and the gateway to the learning resources of the community and the world. This budget, created with the input of students, teachers, parents, and the media advisory committee, furthers the goals of our school and district.

Budget Critique

Note that the budget given is a sample budget. It is not perfect, but can serve as an example (positive and negative). Use the questions below to critique and improve this budget presentation.

- Does it include other people other than the library staff? How many times is the word "I" used?
- Does it refer to specific learning instances?
- Is it short and easily scanned?

- Does it ask for support of initiatives or does it ask for mere monetary support?
- Is it clear who will be hurt by not getting the requested funds?
- Does it have a clear introduction and a clear closing?
- Does it cover equity issues adequately?

Glossary

Alternative Funding Control: The school district budget should be the main support for the school library program. Book fairs, grants, and other types of activities, apart from the school district budget, are alternative funding sources.

Cost Efficiency: The cost of a resource divided by the number of users.

Current Dollars: Refers to the amount that funds budgeted and spent in a previous year would be worth today, adjusting for the annual cost-of-living increases.

Effectiveness: The impact of spending money on a specific target.

Efficiency: Lack of duplication of effort in budget and acquisition processes.

Encumbered: An obligation of the school district to pay for an order not yet received.

Equity: Generally refers to two different types of equality measures; equity of opportunity or equity of outcomes.

Evaluation: Investigating and assessing the process that resulted in the published budget.

Fairness: Free of favoritism or bias. A fair budget process gives equal opportunity to all parties.

Filter: Adding effort to the production function to either enhance value or fix a deviation from the production function.

Financial Policy: The procedures and policies by which a school district manages the budgeting processes.

Fiscal Policy: How a school district views finance policies and the taxpayer/school district relationship.

Fiscal Year: Usually July 1st to June 30th, refers to the budget year.

Funding Adequacy Implementation: The minimum amount of money needed to educate one student.

Implementation: The actual spending of the money in the budget.

Intervention: Economists sometimes refer to this as "interference." It refers to the rules and regulations placed on the free market by government.

Line Items: A budgeted amount for a single item.

Lump Sums: An amount of money placed in a budget from which numerous items, usually of the same type, can be ordered.

Macroeconomics: The big picture of school finance structure.

Market Principles: The economic principles, such as competition, perfect information, etc., that govern an economic relationship between two or more entities.

Matching Grant: An outside funding source pledges an amount of money for the school library, as long as the school district will budget for an equal amount. In the earliest history of school libraries, matching grants between the school district and the state were common. Now most matching grants happen between outside foundation and other grants and the school or school district.

Microeconomics: The details of taxing and spending.

Original Dollars: The actual amount budgeted and reported for a specific year. A mathematical formula adjusts the cost of living annual increases to transform original dollars into what that dollar amount would be in a later year (current dollars).

Per Pupil Allotment: Allocating a set amount of money per enrolled student.

Performance Budgets: A type of budget that makes each program accountable in terms of its effectiveness to the business goal of bottom-line profit.

Planning: Process that results in the published budget.

PPBS: Planning, Programming, Budgeting System was a program-based budget process developed for the Department of Defense.

Production Function: process by which raw materials are transformed into marketable products.

Program Budgets: A type of budget based on the established priorities of the institution.

Reporting: Producing reports and statistics on the budget and acquisitions.

Zero-Based Budgets: A type of budget in which the unit must justify each expenditure, program, and item.

Opportunity Costs: The cost of choosing one activity over another.

Bibliography

Allen, Lew. "From Plaques to Practice: How Schools Can Breathe Life into their Guiding Beliefs." *Phi Delta Kappan*, 83 (4) Dec, 2001: 289-93.

American Association of School Librarians (AASL). *Standards for School Library Programs*. American Library Association. Chicago, 1960.

American Association of School Librarian (AASL)/Association of Educational Communication and Technology (AECT). *Information Power* 2nd ed. Chicago: ALA, 1998.

American Association of School Librarian (AASL)/Association of Educational Communication and Technology (AECT). *Information Power; Guidelines for School Library Media Programs*. Chicago, IL. American Library Association, ©1986.

American Association of School Librarian (AASL)/Association of Educational Communication and Technology (AECT). *Media Programs; District and School*. Chicago, IL. American Library Association, ©1975.

Anderson, Pauline. *Planning School Library Media Facilities*. Hamden, CT: Library Professional Publications, 1990.

Barron, Daniel D. "School-Based Management and School Library Media Specialists." *School Library Media Activities Monthly*, 8. Feb, 1992. p. 47-50.

Bauer, David G. *The Teacher's Guide to Winning Grants*. San Francisco: Jossey-Bass, 1999.

Bomar, Cora Paul "North Carolina School Libraries; A Look at the Past, Present, and Future." *North Carolina Libraries*, 50. 1992: 14-17.

Book Report (serial). Worthington, Ohio: Linworth Publishing, Inc., 1982–2002.

Bosworth, Matthew H. *Courts as Catalyst: State Supreme Courts and Public School Finance Equity*. Albany: State University of New York Press, 2001.

Calahan, Margaret and Elena Hernandez. Statistics of Public and Private School Library Media Centers, 1985-1986, (with historical comparisons from 1958-1985). Center for Educational Statistics. Washington, D.C.: Department of Education. 1987.

Calahan, Raymond E. *Education and the Cult of Efficiency; a Study of the Social Forces That Have Shaped the Administration of the Public Schools.* Univ. of Chicago Press, 1962

Canfield, Jack. *101 Ways to Develop Student Self-Esteem and Responsibility.* Boston: Allyn and Bacon, 1993.

Carver, John. *Creating a Mission That Makes a Difference.* San Francisco. Jossey-Bass. 1997.

Case, Robert N., and Anna Mary Lowrey. *Behavioral Requirements Analysis Checklist; A compilation of competency-based job functions and tasks statements for school library media personnel.* Phase II, School Library Manpower Project. American Association of School Librarians. 1973.

Coleman, James R. *Equity of Educational Opportunity.* Department of Health, Education, and Welfare. Washington, D.C. U.S. Office of Education, c1966.

Covey, Stephen. *The 7 Habits of Highly Effective People; Powerful Lessons for Personal Change.* New York: Simon and Schuster, 1990.

Crowley, John. "A Leadership Role for Teacher-Librarians." *Emergency Librarian,* 22 (5) May-June, 1995: 8-14.

Darling, Richard L. *Public School Library Statistics, 1962-1963.* Washington, D.C: USHEW, 1964.

Dewey, John. "My Pedagogic Creed." *The School Journal, 14,* (2): 77-80. Also published in Dworkin, Martin S. *Dewey on Education.* Teacher's College Press, 1959. p. 19-32. Many of John Dewey's writings are available in the public domain. The School and Society is available through the Internet Public Library. <http://www.ipl.org>.

Dickinson, Gail K. (1987) "History of School Library Supervision in North Carolina." Unpublished master's Thesis. University of North Carolina-Chapel Hill, North Carolina.

Doll, Carol Ann, and Pamela Petrick Barron. *Managing and Analyzing Your Collection*. Chicago:, Ill.: American Library Association, 2002.

Dyson, Robert G. and Frances A. O'Brien (eds.). *Strategic Development; Methods and Models*. Chichester, England: Wiley and Sons, 1998.

Frase, Robert W. "Five Years of Struggle for Federal Funds." Bowker Annual, 1974, p. 156–164.

Gaver, Mary Virginia. *A Braided Cord: Memoirs of a School Librarian*. Metuchen, NJ: Scarecrow, 1988.

Gaver, Mary Virginia. *Effectiveness of Centralized Library Service in Elementary Schools*. Rutgers, The State University, New Brunswick, N.J., 1963.

Gillespie, John T., and Diana L. Spirt. *Administering the School Library Media Center*. New York: Bowker, ©1983.

Goertz, Margaret E., and Allan Odden, eds. *School-based Financing*. Thousand Oaks, CA: Corwin Press, ©1999.

Hall-Ellis, Sylvia D (et al). *Grantsmanship for Small Libraries and School Library Media Centers*. Englewood, CO: Libraries Unlimited, 1999.

Hamilton, Betty. "Site-Based Management and the School Librarian." *Book Report,11*, Jan-Feb, 1993: 20-22.

Hanushek, Eric A. "The Impact of Differential Expenditures on School Performance." *Educational Research*, 18, (4) May 1989: 45-51.

Hartzell, Gary N. "The Invisible School Librarian: Why other educators are blind to your value." *School Library Journal*, 43. November 1997: 24-29.

Hartzell, Gary N. *Building Influence for the School Librarian*. Worthington, Ohio: Linworth Publishing, Inc., 1994.

Hillman, James. *Kinds of Power; A guide to its intelligent uses*. New York: Bantam, 1995.

Hughes-Hassell, Sandra and Anne Wheelock (eds). *The Information-Powered School*. Public Education Network and the American Association of School Librarians. Chicago: American Library Association, 2001.

Kearney, Carol A. *Curriculum Partner; Redefining the Role of the Library Media Specialist*. Greenwood, 2000.

Kids Who Read … Succeed. (slogan). American Library Association (ALA) Web site. <www.ALA.org>. Accessed 5/21/02.

Klasing, Jane P. *Designing and Renovating Library Media Centers*. Chicago, IL: ALA, 1991.

Krashen, Stephen D. *The Power of Reading; Insights from the Research*. Englewood, CO.:Libraries Unlimited, 1993.

Kreiser, Latane C, and John Hortin. "The History of the Curriculum Integrated Library Media Program Concept." *International Journal of Instructional Media*, 19, (4). 1992: 313-330.

Ladd, Helen F., and Janet S. Hansen. *Making money matter: Financing America's Schools*. Committee on Education Finance, Commission on Behavioral and Social Sciences and Education, National Research Council. Washington, D.C.: National Academy Press, ©1999.

Library Advocacy Now was an initiative beginning with the ALA president Patricia Glass Schuman. Schuman's efforts provided money for training, and for materials. The @ Your Library program is the current ALA advocacy initiative. Information can be found about these programs on the ALA Web site at www.ala.org.

McKinzie, Steve. "Hell to Pay: The Dark Side of Advocacy." *Journal of Information Ethics*, 10, no. 1, Spring 2001: 5-7.

Miller, Marilyn L. and Barbara Moran. "Expenditures for Resources in School Library Media Centers, FY '82-'83." *School Library Journal*, October, 1983. p. 105–114.

Miller, Marilyn L. and Barbara Moran. "Expenditures for Resources in School Library Media Centers, FY '83-'84." *School Library Journal*, October, 1985. p. 19–30.

Miller, Marilyn L. and Barbara Moran. "Expenditures for Resources in School Library Media Centers FY '85-'86." *School Library Journal*, June-July, 1987. p. 37–45.

Miller, Marilyn L and Marilyn L. Shontz. "Expenditures for Resources in School Library Media Center FY 1988-1989." *School Library Journal*, June, 1989. p. 31–40.

Miller, Marilyn L and Marilyn L. Shontz. "Expenditures for Resources in School Library Media Center FY 1989-1990." *School Library Journal*, August, 1991. p. 32–38

Miller, Marilyn L. and Marilyn L. Shontz. "Expenditures for Resources in School Library Media Center FY 1991-1992." *School Library Journal*, October, 1993. p. 26-36.

Miller, Marilyn L and Marilyn L. Shontz. "How Do You Measure Up?" *School Library Journal*, October, 1999. p. 50-59.

Miller, Marilyn L. and Marilyn L. Shontz. "The Race for the School Library Dollar; Expenditures for Resources in School Library Media Centers, FY 1993-1994." *School Library Journal*, October, 1995. p. 22-33.

Miller, Marilyn L. and Marilyn L. Shontz. "New Money, Old Books." *School Library Journal*, October, 2001. p. 50-62.

Miller, Marilyn L. and Marilyn L. Shontz. "Small Change: Expenditures for Resources in School Library Media Centers, FY 1995-1996." *School Library Journal*, October, 1997. p. 28-37.

Morris, Paul. *A Practical Guide to Fund-Raising in Schools*. New York: Routledge, 2000.

Odden, Allen and Carolyn Busch. *Financing schools for high performance: strategies for improving the use of educational resources*. San Francisco: Jossey-Bass, ©1998.

Porter, G. Margaret. "What Does Electronic Access to Bibliographic Information Cost?" *College and Research Libraries News*, no. 2, Feb, 1991: 90-92.

Rebore, William T. and Ronald W. Rebore. *Introduction to Financial and Business Administration in Public Education*. Boston, MA: Allyn and Bacon, ©1993.

Schement, Jorge Reina. "Imagining Fairness; Equality and Equity of Access in Search of Democracy." In ... Nancy Kranich, Libraries and Democracy; the Cornerstones of Liberty. Chicago: ALA, 2001.

Simon, Paul. "The Federal Role in Support of School Library Media Programs." *School Library Media Annual.* Vol. 13, 1995: 4-6.

Trelease, Jim. *The Read-Aloud Handbook.* New York: Penguin, 1982.

Turner, Anne M. *Getting Political; an action guide for librarians and library supporters.* New York: Neal-Schuman, 1997.

Verstegen, Deborah A. "The New Wave of School Finance Litigation." *Phi Delta Kappan*, 76 (3). November, 1994: 243-250.

Wallace, Linda K. *Library Advocate's Handbook.* American Library Association, 2000.

Walters, Suzanne. *Marketing; A how-to-do-it manual for librarians.* New York: Neal-Schuman, 1992.

Weingand, Darlene E. *Marketing/Planning Library and Information Services.* Littleton, CO., Libraries Unlimited, 1987.

Zweizig, Douglas L., and Dianne McAfee Hopkins. *Lessons from Library Power; Enriching Teaching and Learning.* Libraries Unlimited, c1999.

Index

Access 13, 17, 32, 62, 77, 109, 134
Accountability 4-6, 51-52, 55, 118
Advocacy 60, 67-78, 87, 119
Alternative Funding Sources 12, 38, 138-140
Audiovisual resources 20, 98, 107-108, 126-127
Average Book Price 36, 104-106
Behavior Requirements Analysis Checklist 18-20
Block grants 22-25
Bomar, Cora Paul 16-17
Budget functions (planning, implementing, evaluating, reporting) 42, 46-49
Bureau of Labor Statistics CPI 33-37
Categorical aid 21-22
Change processes 7-9, 12-15
Callahan, Raymond 45
Coleman Report 57
Collection Analysis 93-96, 120
Committee for Full Funding of Education Programs 19, 21
Conference expenses 86, 98-99
Covey, Stephen 7, 109-110
Current Dollars (formula) 28, 33-35
Department of Education Surveys 23, 27-30
Dewey, John 9, 141
Dewey, Melvil 16
Dickinson, Jr., Charles W. 16
Diversity issues 84
Electronic resources 6, 31, 111-112, 121, 124, 127-8, 140
Encumbering of funds 43
Equipment 22, 24, 26, 43-44, 98-99, 107, 127-128
ESEA 17-22
Facilities 92, 96
Flexible access 75
Ford Fantasy Project 18
Funding adequacy 60-61
Gaver, Mary Virginia 16-19
Government Intervention in Markets 56
Grantwriting 12, 38, 139-140

Hanushek, Eric 58, 60
Hartzell, Gary 75-76
Henne, Frances 18
Historical overview of expenditures 24-32
Information curriculum 56, 75
Information Power 9, 57, 76, 87-88, 90, 121
Knapp School Library Project 18-19
Library Power 12, 90
Magazines 87, 97, 99, 102,
Market theory 54-58
Matching funds 17, 91
Mathews, Virginia 18
Media Advisory Committee 80, 139
Mission 9-12
Opportunity cost 137-138
Original Dollars 12, 32-37
Parent relationships 9, 67, 71-75, 77, 91, 108
Performance-based budgets 51
PPBS 50
Principal-Library Interaction 8, 64, 75, 89-90, 121
Production Function 56-61
Program budgets 50-51
Reading 6, 57, 60, 82, 84, 97, 106, 123
Regional Accreditation Standards 88-89
School and Staffing Survey 24
School-based management 49
School Library Manpower Project 18
School Library Media Production Function 59
School-public library relationships 55-56
School Reform 45-49
Site-Based Management 45-48
Staffing 91
Standards 16-17, 29, 86-90
Statistics 27-37
Supplies 30, 99, 128
Visioning 9-13
Volunteers 91, 138
Zero-based budgets 49-50

About the Author

Gail Dickinson started her career as a K-12 school library media specialist in Cape Charles, Virginia. She has been library media specialist at public and private schools, a library supervisor, and is now serves as assistant professor and coordinator of school library media at the University of North Carolina at Greensboro.

Originally from the mountains of south central Pennsylvania, she has lived on the coast of Virginia, upstate New York, and the North Carolina piedmont. She has an undergraduate degree in educational media from Millersville University in Pennsylvania, an MLS from the University of North Carolina at Chapel Hill, and a PhD in educational administration from the University of Virginia. She has been interested in budget and expenditures for school library media for almost a decade. Other research interests include the National Board for Professional Teaching Standards and other issues of school library management.

An avid sports fan and accomplished couch potato, she has recently added NASCAR to her football and basketball interests. She divides her time between Greensboro, North Carolina, and Smith's Beach, Virginia.

www.ingramcontent.com/pod-product-compliance
Lightning Source LLC
Chambersburg PA
CBHW081154290426
44108CB00018B/2552